W9-BQT-536

LUMBERING IN EARLY TWENTIETH CENTURY MICHIGAN

THE KNEELAND-BIGELOW COMPANY EXPERIENCE

By Herman Lunden Miller

Literary Rights Reserved

April 15, 1995

Second Edition, 2007

Second Edition
Published by Walnut Hill Press
P.O. Box 842
Lewiston, Michigan 49756

Designed by Bauer Dunham & Barr

ISBN 0-9645716-0-9

CONTENTS

Illustrations List

Illustration List, Page 2

PREFACE

As pine lumbering in Michigan neared its end early in the twentieth century, large areas of hardwood and hemlock, sometimes mixed with pine, still stood north of Saginaw Bay. This book describes one large lumber company's experience and methods while lumbering some of those areas. The first six chapters describe how the Kneeland-Bigelow (KB) Company developed and how it bought, managed, and sold its timberlands. Later chapters describe its mills briefly, but its methods of logging at length. The text concludes with a description of the stock farm and the end of logging. KB logged and retained ownership of most of its land with the intention of logging again when the second growth had matured. However, plans for such sustained yield management were frustrated and this book tells why.

My grandfather, Herman Lunden, ran KB's woods and farming operations. His idea of managing for sustained yield grew out of his father's experience in Sweden. He was an ardent conservationist, serving on the first Michigan Conservation Commission in 1923-6. His papers were kept and became the basis for this book, along with my interviews with men and women who had worked for KB. The files had at least one letter from and to the company president, Charles Bigelow, almost every working day, making possible a detailed history. Unfortunately, there were several years without any correspondence or information. There was no correspondence with the earlier company president, David Kneeland, before 1911. Probably, this was because his home was only one block from Lunden's home in Lewiston. The files are now at the Bentley Historical Library of the University of Michigan in Ann Arbor except for some I have retained and my interview notes.

I grew up in Herman Lunden's former home, 0.7 mile south of the KB logging headquarters, surrounded by miles of mostly KB land. I went to school with the children of the men who had worked for KB. My mother liked to talk about the lumbering days, and had stored Herman Lunden's correspondence files in the garage and attic.

Everyone I asked about KB was very helpful. Besides those mentioned in the references, the following contributed information: Albert Blixberg, Frank Currie, Louise Doyle, Kenneth Scheffel, and Irene Warsaw.

An album of 1910 KB photographs by John D. Cress was loaned by David Kneeland who then gave them to Michigan Historical Collections, Bentley Historical Library, University of Michigan. The superb photographs made in 1925 by William Kuenzel are reprinted with permission of The Detroit News, a Gannett newspaper, copyright 1925. Kenneth Chadwick arranged for me to get copies of some of the photographs in the George H. Vincent collection. June Chadwick let me copy several photographs from Kenneth Chadwick's collection. John H. Lunden let me use several photographs. Thomas Young assisted with copies from his collection.

Much of Part I was published in Forest and Conservation History, January 1992, p. 22.

Fred White contributed greatly with encouragement, answering countless questions, and making sketches of sleighs, jammers, Russell logging cars, and the KB Store. The amount of his contribution can be gauged by the 21 references that have his name out of a total of 133.

Four of Fred White's sketches were made into printable form by Scott Casper and two by Roberta Capistrant.

Professor James Waltz of Eastern Michigan University carefully read the manuscript in draft form and provided helpful suggestions for its revision.

Thomas L. Jones arranged for Professor Waltz to read the manuscript and in other ways assisted with editing, making many suggestions that were incorporated. He helped get the book into final form and met with book designers.

My wife, Dorothy, helped me gather data, tolerated my long preoccupation with this book, read it critically and made suggestions that were incorporated.

Part I of this book is about how the KB Company developed, its organization, management, finances, problems, and how its goal of sustained yield forestry ended. If these seem uninteresting, one can skip to Part II, which tells how the company did its logging and milling--similarly to other lumber companies at the time and so of general interest.

Second Edition 2007 Preface

The Second edition has been enlarged by adding a list of illustrations, a photograph of a blacksmith in the shop at Camp 4, and a description of a big saw mill and planing mill. The mills were located at Rapid River, about fifteen miles north of Escanaba and being offered for sale by Wm. Haywood in a 1927 letter to Herman Lunden. Apparently. every piece of equipment necessary for operation is described. which makes it of historical interest.

Short additions that could not be easily fitted into the text follow here:

An additional cause of sawmill fires were the moving belts transmitting mechanical power through the mills and generating electrical sparks that would ignite sawdust.

Another reason for employing journeyman carpenters to build the big barn was that the trusses for a gambrel roof are complicated and a challenge for carpenters.

Part I

The Company Experience

Corporate Development

The Kneeland-Bigelow (KB) Company, incorporated on May 29, 1901[1], was very much a company of the new twentieth century, distinctly different from its pine era predecessors. Its founders were managers and stockholders of the Michelson & Hanson Lumber Company (M&H), a mostly pine operation with mills in Lewiston, Michigan. Something—perhaps fear of running out of timber—made all of the M&H management team look for new positions during 1901. They were part of group associated with Rasmus Hanson of Grayling for many years previously. David M. Kneeland[2] was treasurer and general manager of M&H and continued in that position until M&H ended operations in 1910. He provided a majority of KB capital and was its president until his death on December 8, 1915. Charles A. Bigelow, the M&H corporate secretary and traveling salesman, became KB's first secretary-treasurer and general manager. Eventually he became president and Walter N. Wrape became secretary-treasurer. In 1901, Herman Lunden was M&H's sawmill superintendent and land looker (timber buyer) and became KB vice president after some months, when the KB logging operation faltered.[3] In addition, he and George Cross had been running a small hardwood logging operation in the SW 1/4 of Section 25, six miles north of Lewiston.

M&H sold its hardwood and hemlock timberlands north of Lewiston to KB with price and terms favorable to KB, which got a good start that way. The land yielded an average of 12,000 board-feet per acre plus valuable hemlock bark.[4] A close relationship between KB and M&H was shown by Kneeland and Lunden remaining on the M&H board of directors until that corporation dissolved in 1912. Kneeland moved people between the two companies as needed. I really found no satisfactory explanation of why M&H sold its hardwood and hemlock timber north of Lewiston to KB instead of cutting it. I asked my relatives why M&H did not log their hardwood timber themselves, and the answer was always, "They were pine people." The old pine lumbermen were so proud of the superb pine lumber that they did not want to condescend to cut lesser trees. Nevertheless, M&H did cut hardwood that went to the Kerry and Hanson flooring mill in Grayling. (For example, during 1901, M&H sold 1,118,871 board-feet of hardwood lumber and 11,727,009 board-feet of hemlock from a total of 31,018,219 board-feet sold.)[5] Some land M&H sold to KB was considered too hilly to be logged profitably. The hills six and more miles north of Lewiston probably appeared daunting to men accustomed to harvesting logs over a dense network of narrow gauge railroads on level ground. It seems as if Messrs. Michelson and Hanson wanted to help start KB, perhaps because they were simultaneously starting Johannesburg Manufacturing Company. M&H stockholders who did not participate in the KB venture started the Johannesburg Manufacturing Company, a relatively small hardwood cutting, sawmill and veneer mill operation ten miles northwest of Lewiston.[6]

KB's timber resources were too widely scattered (see map) to justify building a sawmill and narrow gauge railroad system as M&H and others had done earlier. It made more sense economically to build onto the standard-gauge common-carrier railroad network and have the logs hauled 130 to 150 miles to existing saw mills in Bay City. In 1901, Bay City mills were cheap because almost no timber remained nearby. There was also a large labor supply, including skilled sawmill men. Because railroad rates for logs were less than for lumber, the product moved part way to its market, mostly south of Bay City, at cheaper rates. Bay City was still an important sawmill center as late as March 30, 1912, when *The American Lumberman* estimated that its mills all together required 100 carloads of logs per day.

KB started at a good time because the market for northern Michigan hardwoods developed at the turn of the century. The reasons for this are:

1. Depletion of hardwood timber in southern Michigan
2. Use of hardwood in automobile bodies, frames, and wheels earlier used in carriages, wagons, and railroad cars
3. Growth of the furniture manufacturing industry
4. Increasing use of power tools to reduce manufacturing costs and make furniture, etc. more affordable to a larger market
5. Greater popularity of hardwood floors
6. Wider demand for bowling pins and alleys

All of the preceding were important to KB's success. Automobile body manufacturers bought most of KB's hardwoods in 1928.[7]

At the time KB was operating, there were only two other comparable lumber manufacturers in northern Michigan, the W. H. White Company of Boyne City and Cobb and Mitchell, Inc. of Cadillac. Cobb & Mitchell finished its cut in 1925. The White company went bankrupt a year or two later[8], without finishing its cut. It had operated along the Boyne City, Gaylord, and Alpena Railroad, (BCG&ARR), owned by the Whites. In Montmorency County, KB usually operated south of the BCG&ARR. There were many companies smaller than KB.

KB soon grew so successful that its stockholders could invest in other lumbering companies. In 1905, some KB stockholders bought the Wylie-Buell (formally, Wylie and Buell Lumber Company) Bay City sawmill and combined it with Frank Buell's timber lands and logging operation in Otsego County to form the Kneeland, Buell & Bigelow Company (KBB). In 1911, this firm became the Kneeland, Lunden & Bigelow Company (KLB) with the same officers as KB. Its operations expanded from Otsego County into Cheboygan, Antrim, and Charlevoix counties. Originally, KB cutting operations were limited to Montmorency and Oscoda counties. Soon after KLB merged into KB in 1922, it expanded to Chippewa and Luce Counties in the Upper Peninsula. In 1922, the Kneeland-Bigelow Trust was organized to hold title to cutover lands; additional lands were transferred to the trust as their logging was completed.

In 1916, some KB stockholders purchased the Cooper flooring mill in Bay City, and operated it as the Bigelow-Cooper Company until 1922, when it merged into KB along with KLB. The merger brought together companies that all had about the same stockholders and were headed by Charles Bigelow. The original investment in KB was $70,000 in 1901, in KLB it was $100,000 in 1905, and in Bigelow-Cooper it was $320,000 in 1916.

David Kneeland also was president of the Grayling Lumber Company in Monroe, Louisiana, from 1910 to 1912. Then he and Percy S. McLurg (General Manager of Grayling Lumber) left to start the Kneeland-McLurg Lumber Company in Wisconsin. The new company had about the same ownership and officers as KB, with the addition of McLurg. It was slightly larger than KB was after 1922. Its sawmills in Phillips and Morse, each equipped with a double band saw and two resaws and electrically driven throughout, started operation in 1912.[9] Kneeland-McLurg liquidated from 1929 to 1938. Kneeland was also president of the Kneeland-West Lumber Company of Lugerville, Wisconsin, organized in April 1914.[10] He spent less of his time on KB than on the other companies. In 1928, C. A. Bigelow had been president of Kneeland-McLurg for some

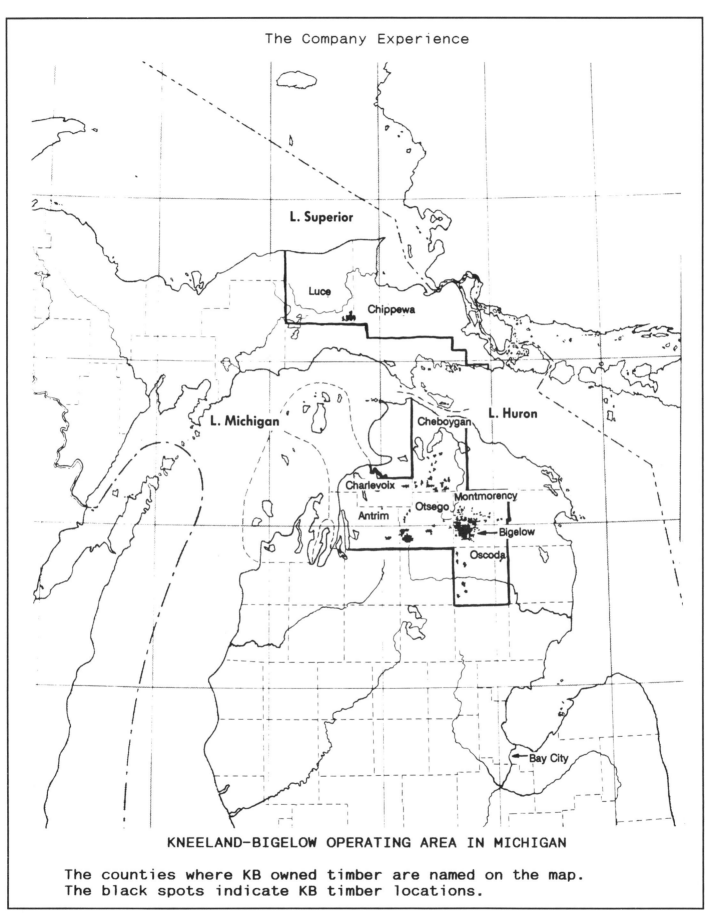

The Company Experience

L. Superior

Luce

Chippewa

L. Michigan

Cheboygan

L. Huron

Charlevoix

Montmorency

Otsego

Antrim

← Bigelow

Oscoda

← Bay City

KNEELAND-BIGELOW OPERATING AREA IN MICHIGAN

The counties where KB owned timber are named on the map.
The black spots indicate KB timber locations.

Kneeland-Bigelow operating area in Michigan.

time,[11] while Pierson Kneeland was the every-day manager at Phillips.

After the merger in 1922, the KB stock owner-ship was as follows:

D. M. Kneeland heirs:	61.6%;
C. A. Bigelow and wife:	25.6%;
Herman Lunden and heirs:	6.1%;
George and Mary Holmes:	3.3%;
Walter N. Wrape:	3.1%;
Others:	0.7%

Bigelow managed the companies by writing frequent letters stating what he wanted done or demanding information. He did not, however, visit the logging operations or familiarize him-self with them. No mention of any visit occurs in the correspondence. Nevertheless, Lunden had to defend himself continually against Bigelow's criticisms and attempts to micro-manage. For instance, Bigelow suggested to Lunden that he replace a well-paid supervisor with one of his lesser paid subordinates. Lunden balked at this, so Bigelow admonished him: "You must not think it dishonorable to let a man out, even though he has been with us a long time, providing of course, we have no work which he can do, [Generally true, but that was not the situation.] but it is dishonorable to your partners and the stockholders to keep a man employed simply because he has been with us a long time."[12] Apparently, Bigelow did keep Lunden informed about activities in the sawmills, and particularly about sale of lands. Probably, Bigelow was frustrated by KB's con-tinuing unprofitability after 1923. He suffered from diabetes, which got out of control in 1928 and caused severe weight loss, putting him in Detroit's Harper Hospital from the end of July until Thanksgiving. It seems unlikely that KB would have succeeded and grown during its early years, if Bigelow had behaved then as he did during its latter years. Despite Bigelow's exasperating personality and shoot-from-the-hip management style, his associates evidently had considerable regard for him: They donated the company's land on the Middle Ground (an island just upstream from the Water Street mill) to Bay City for a park in his honor.

Corporate Operations and Costs

The lumber industry was (and still is) highly competitive because one company's board is about the same as any other company's of the same grade and species, assuming proper milling. A railroad carload of lumber could be shipped economically almost anywhere, so prices could not get too high locally. Therefore lumber companies had to be both frugal and efficient or they soon went broke, as many did. KB accountants produced balance sheets every month and put great effort into knowing its costs, so KB survived to finish its cut, with minor exceptions. (KB carried frugality so far that the office staff cut up used envelopes and stapled them together into memo pads rather than buying new pads.)

In 1923, the first year after the merger, KB made a profit of $53,365, which is 1.9% on sales of $2,848,813 and 1.35% on assets of $3,946,123, not an attractive performance. The performance would have appeared better if timber depletion had not been taken into account. At the end of 1923, assets included $1,780,264 of timberlands; $1,096,813 of mills, camps, equipment, and farms; plus current assets of $953,572. There were notes payable of $491,000, but no long-term debt.

The year 1925 was difficult for KB and the lumber industry generally, despite the stock market's strong rise. Volume and prices of for-est products sold decreased, so the industry responded with layoffs and wage cuts. KB reduced sawmill costs, but its return on lumber was much less than that of 1924. Bigelow reduced overhead by $51,051, but KB still lost $121,915 during the year. Generally, strong pressure exists to continue unprofitable opera-tions while their cash flow remains positive, even in an extractive industry like lumbering. But during such operation, a company's exist-ing resources become depleted, and money is not available to purchase new resources. Clearly, a company could not long continue to operate in this fashion.

Herman Lunden thought that lumber prices were depressed in 1927 because several compa-nies had come almost to the end of their timber and wanted to finish their cut quickly, without regard to profitability, a situation similar to that at KB.[13] (In retrospect, these conditions seem to be forerunners of the Great Depression.) Another indicator of the difficult economy was the bankruptcy of W. H. White & Company under the same capable management that had run it since 1886.

During the 1920s, logging cost KB from $5 to $20 per thousand board feet, depending on conditions. The average cost for cutting, skidding, hauling, decking (piling), and loading logs, per thousand board-feet during 1928 was:

Camp 2, southwest of Gaylord,	$10.271
Camp 20, north of Rexton,	$16.818
Camp 22, east of Gaylord,	$11.616

Indirect costs (mostly depletion) raised the above costs to an average total cost of $24.813 loaded on cars in the woods. The average cost of log freight to the sawmill was $6.150 per thousand board-feet. Sawmill and lumber yard costs (mostly labor) were $6.732 per thousand board-feet, reduced to $4.055 by firewood sales. These data show that the biggest cost was cutting and moving the logs (each weighing approximately one ton) to the railroad and loading them on cars. Adding to the above, the costs of moving lumber from the sawmill to the flooring mill and finishing it resulted in an average final flooring cost of $60.257 per thousand board-feet in 1928 and average selling price of $63.628 per thousand.[14] Persistent rain in 1928 made logging costs higher than usual, particularly in the UP, where operating conditions went from difficult to impossible, forcing temporary shutdown of Camp 20.

In contrast, the year ending October 31, 1907, showed much lower costs. The KBB sawmill ran 2884.75 hours with an average of 6972 board-feet/hour. Slabs (the first and last slices) from softwood logs were made into lath, while edges and slabs from hardwood were cut into firewood. Profit from firewood and lath sales was shown as a negative cost.[15]

Costs per thousand board-feet were:

	KBB	KB
	1907	1928
Average cost of logs on cars	$6.85	$24.81
Average cost of log freight	$2.27	$6.15
Cost of sawing lumber	$2.24	$6.73
Lumber yard work		$0.38
General and administrative	$1.08	
Profit from wood & lath sales	$-1.27	$-2.68
Total cost of lumber	$11.55	$35.02
Average sale price (excluding flooring)	$15.36	$41.00

Somewhat comparable data on costs of lumbering nearby in 1913, 1919, and 1920 are available for Johannesburg Manufacturing.[16]

KB and Johannesburg Manufacturing were the last Lower Peninsula sawmill and timber owning companies to employ their own logging crews.[17] Other companies changed earlier to contracting with jobbers for all cutting. On small tracts, swamp timber, and running a railroad tie mill, KB had been contracting with jobbers for several years. The reasons for contracting logging included:

- Camp costs increased over the years, so by 1927, KB needed a timber block well over 1000 acres to justify building a company camp, but such tracts had become very rare.
- The company no longer needed to have men available to defend its timber against fire, because the State had assumed that responsibility.
- Settling of the countryside and development of towns eliminated the need for an organization to supply and support camps in the wilderness.
- More available roads and greater usability of trucks with trailers instead of railroads to haul logs.
- Corporate overhead charges were avoided when jobbers cut timber, because they did not receive the costly supervision and support provided foremen. Lunden said, "We cannot make money under the present expensive system of doing business. No block of timber could stand $50,000 of overhead," the amount of KB officers' annual salaries.[18]

(Left): Maple timber on SW NW 16, 30N-2E southeast of Big Rock, 1910.

(Right): Five foot diameter elm tree near Camp 10, NW SW 16, 30N-2E, 1910.

Bigelow and Lunden debated the question of having all KB logging done by jobbers. Bigelow cited figures that seemed to show substantial savings by using jobbers. Lunden countered that the cited figures did not include the cost of building spur railroads because that was done by other contractors. KB crews built at least the grades for its spur railroads. Logging costs would appear unduly low on level ground where railroad spurs could be close together and no sleigh roads were built. Lunden, who had an excellent grasp of his costs, believed his logging costs were really below others: "Ross and Wentworth get $8.50 per thousand logging because they do not charge any taxes against it and only part of railroad construction."[19] Unless someone had a more efficient method or better equipment, cost savings by jobbing over direct company operations were illusory, but might show up differently in accounting. As importantly, direct control of logging helped to minimize damage to uncut trees.

Acquisition of Timberlands

KB got its timber lands from several sources; including earlier lumber companies, speculators, and farmers. Buying timber aggressively and years ahead of need assured the company's long-term existence. In March 1904, KB estimated[20] that it still had 31,787,000 bd-ft of hemlock out of 80,179,000 bd-ft of all species left to cut on its land five to ten miles north of Lewiston. KB purchased additional land north of Lewiston from the Salling family of Manistee in June 1904 and July 1905.[21] By 1910, KB and KLB owned approximately 27,500 acres of land carrying 700,000,000 board-feet, in addition to timber rights on about 15,000 acres carrying about 300,000,000 board-feet.[22] In March 1912, KLB paid $225,000 for 3440 acres from the David Ward Estate[23] a large pine lumbering operation that had just ended its cut. Located on the Detroit and Charlevoix Railroad in Otsego County, it was estimated to contain 70,000,000 board-feet of mixed, merchantable timber. Other well-financed companies competed to buy the timber. After that purchase, KB and

Photo by Wm. Kuenzel

Timber along road to new Camp 2, SW of Gaylord, 1925.

KLB were reported to have 30,000 acres of timber.[24] In 1915, KB purchased the timber on 1720 acres from J. M. Peterson. In fact, between 1913 and 1923, KB and KLB made 38 purchases totaling 5535 acres, mostly of timber without the land, so the two firms cut at least 20,000 acres where they owned only the timber. In 1923, KB purchased from Mershon-Morley a 7040-acre Upper Peninsula (UP) tract estimated to contain 38,509,000 board-feet and from Allen A. Atwood, an adjoining tract of 1240 acres, estimated to contain 3,722,000 board-feet. Considerable swamp timber was present, but it was not included in the estimates for the tracts. In 1924, KB purchased a 960-acre tract six miles east of Gaylord, from the Standard Hoop Company, a manufacturer of barrel hoops. KB also purchased a tract in T33N-R1W of southeastern Cheboygan County from Henry Germaine.

Before a buyer purchased timber, a timber cruiser went over the land and estimated how much of each species were on it, and the cost to log it, so the buyer would know how much he could afford to pay. The cruiser recorded data in leather-bound books with a format printed for that specific purpose. Lumber companies maintained timber estimate or "cruise books" that showed the number of board feet of each species in each quarter-quarter section (forty acres) of land they owned. KB's cruise books still exist. The company's strategy was to buy timber that was cheap just because it was on hilly ground and would be expensive to log. This strategy reduced the interest and tax cost of holding the timber until cutting, but caused larger cutting costs. KB bought some Ward Estate timber land that neither Stephens Lumber Company nor Salling Hanson would buy at any price.[25] Evidently, KB had economical techniques for logging hilly ground because it stayed in business.

KB was still purchasing timber, but in small blocks, during the 1920s. Farmers satisfied with their land sold only the timber in order to clear more land for farming. Farmers dissatisfied with their land simply sold it and moved to more promising areas. (Settlers began homesteading in Otsego and Montmorency counties during the 1870s, but lacking a hardwood market they had to burn the hardwood logs when they cleared land.) KB's timber lands were exclusively in Michigan, although Lunden did make three trips to the Pacific coast to look at timber for KB, but the company did not make any purchases there.[26]

Sustained Yield

Nineteenth century lumbermen had expected that their cutover lands would eventually become farms. By 1901, this expectation was proving false for northern Michigan pine lands which were usually on sandy and acid soil. Although much of KB's hardwood land was clay suitable for farming—and some did become successful farms—the company expected most of its cutover land to continue to grow trees. Usually, KB retained its lands and paid taxes until the land was sold. Originally, KB did this with the expectation of sustained yields, so that the land could be logged again in about thirty years (a strategy feasible with northern hardwoods, but not pine). Unfortunately, KB and KLB did not acquire enough land to carry out this plan, although they did own more than 50,000 acres by the time they began trying to sell land in 1925.[27] They ran out of virgin timber before their second growth matured enough to cut. Moreover, although KB owned almost 23,000 contiguous acres in Montmorency County, the rest of its land was scattered in smaller tracts that would have been expensive to manage.

It is worth noting that early in this century, few if any companies in the United States were managing hardwood lands for sustained yield. Johannesburg Manufacturing clearcut completely, but most of their land was suitable for farming. The Dierks lumber companies operating in the Ouachita area of Arkansas and Oklahoma with an area of 900,000 acres were successful in sustained yield management of southern pine.[28] Part of their success, however, required making a great effort to prevent forest fires.

To pursue his goal of sustained yield, Lunden set strict limits on minimum- diameter trees to be cut (eight inches at smaller end, twelve inches at the stump), and required careful cutting to minimize damage to young trees nearby, so the land could be lumbered repeatedly. The woodcutters, who cleaned up after the logging, were strictly limited to cutting tops and damaged trees, leaving the good, straight trees to grow.[29] The KB cutting policy was successful for hardwoods, but not for hemlock, which gave dense shade that prevented growth of seedlings. Cutting pure hemlock stands left barren ground that usually became aspen or sumac covered, while mixed hardwood and hemlock stands converted to second-growth hardwood, so now there is almost no hemlock growing.

Lunden also believed strongly that the residue of tops should be left to rot and not be burned. He came to this belief after working in the Michigan lumber woods since in 1880 and traveling enough to see both the effects of, and recovery from, the big forest fires of those years. Excerpts from a speech he gave about 1927 state the reasons for his view on this still controversial subject:

> People who say "burn the slash" do not know what they are talking about, for I am here to tell you that from many years of experience in this work, I am a firmer believer every year that the slash should not be burned. Particularly is this true of hardwood. The main reason that it should not be burned is the very fact that the burning kills the young timber, burns the humus in the soil, the limbs and tops that give protection to the young timber, and increases rather than decreases the fire hazard. . . . I have always found that the second fire [on a tract] is worse than the first one. I can show you today fine tracts of second growth hardwood, where the merchantable timber was cut twenty-five years ago, which now have much good merchantable timber on them. I personally lumbered much of this and know that the slash was not burned, yet there is no sign of it now, and there has not been for years. It rotted and went back to earth to form a mulch and soil humus that assisted the young timber, which was there to grow when the large timber was cut. I can show you other tracts where the slash was burned and natural reproduction has never taken place. . . . allowing weeds, brush and briars to grow and choke out the trees that might have sprouted there.

> . . . I can show you places where once were large swamps of virgin swamp timber, which were burned over after the first harvest of timber was completed, where now nothing but brush and tall swamp grasses are growing. On the other hand, I can show you—in the same territory—where swamps of large and fine swamp timber have been cut and they are still producing merchantable timber because the fire has been kept out. At the present time, we are cutting swamp timber in a swamp that we cut only a few years ago. We have kept the fires out, and today we are cutting a good grade of swamp timber. It cost us much less to keep the fires out than it would have cost to burn the slash and plant seedlings. If we had burned the slash and planted seedlings, it would still have been necessary to keep the fires out, and would have taken a much longer time to have produced the timber. . . . These things which have come under my personal observation have caused me more and more to grow away from all programs of reforestation to produce merchantable timber, and become more and more convinced that . . . the prevention of fire in our present timber areas is the one surest and quickest way of getting back the great stands of timber we once had.[30]

KB logged some second-growth red (Norway) pine, so Lunden had evidence that it would grow back without being planted. During a 1925 inspection of original KB holdings in Montmorency County, logged during 1901 to 1910, Colonel W. B. Greeley, Chief of the U.S. Forest Service, felt they were the outstanding example of second growth hardwood and was convinced of the value of natural reforestation.[31] The tract was logged again in 1935-37, then everything remaining was cut for chemical wood, thus aborting Lunden's plan for sustained yield. Nevertheless, in the years preceeding that relogging, KB management made a vigorous effort to sell the tract to persons who would manage it on a sustained yield basis, but failed to find a buyer. Where the soil is good and a timber stand improvement cut was done, the timber has recovered from clear-cutting so it probably would be worth logging about 2004. (Some KB timber has been preserved in the wide right-of-way for highway M-32 across Vienna township in southwestern Montmorency county, where fresh green in the spring, and red and gold in the fall, delight travelers every year.)

Sale of Timberlands

The justification for not continuing to hold the timberlands was explained in a speech H. Lunden gave about the Timberland Tax Law to the Tri-State Development Conference in Duluth, January 24, 1925:

Some twenty years ago, our company decided to make a strong effort to protect a certain tract of land that was then being lumbered for saw timber and chemical wood, from fire. We did not allow the woodcutters to cut any young standing timber for wood, as we wanted to know what the result would be.

On an average, this land will now cut 2000 feet of saw log timber per acre, worth not less than $20.00 or $10.00 per acre stumpage. This same acre will cut at least 14 cords of chemical wood at 75 cents per cord [stumpage] which amounts to $10.50 per acre, or a total revenue per acre of $30.50. The average charges against this land are as follows: The lands were placed at a value of $6.00 per acre, which at 6% [compounded annually] for twenty years would amount to $19.18 [for interest]. The taxes, which have been about 22 cents per acre for twenty years plus interest would amount to $8.60. Fire protection at 5 cents per acre for 20 years plus interest would amount to $1.95 making a total of $29.73 or a net gain of 77 cents per acre. The taxes at present are higher than when this land was set aside and consequently, it would not show a profit now. This, of course, is not taking in overhead expense, [fire]tower building, telephone system, etc. and with that added, you can see that it would be a loss to the owner to try to raise timber. However, if the taxes had been placed at 5 cents per acre on the reforestry land, it would have made a small profit to

the owner, but owing to the fact that taxes would be raised yearly faster than the growth of the timber, it cannot be raised successfully by private owners without some assurance of [solving] the tax problem.[30]

The Michigan Commercial Forest Reserve Act, passed in 1925, was not as generous as Lunden had hoped, so one could foresee the end of KB in Lunden's calculation showing little or no profit in holding timberland. During 1925, KB's policy changed from occasional passive selling of cutover land if people sought it, to aggressive efforts to dispose of all such land. Nevertheless, Lunden wrote that he would not sell unproductive land to people for farming.[32] He also wrote, "I started reserving mineral, oil and gas rights a long time ago."[33] If there is ever production, the rights are worth much more than the surface, so it behooves the seller to retain the rights. As another step in the process of land disposal, the Kneeland-Bigelow Trust deeded 1920 acres in T33N-R3W, west of Wolverine, to the State as a gift in 1925. Other companies also saw no future in owning land. For example, Cobb and Mitchell in December 1924, made a much larger gift of 38,000 acres to the State, followed some 14 months later by another gift of 1200 acres west of Wolverine.[34] In July 1927, KB deeded a tract along the Sturgeon River for public use.[35] The remaining KB lands in southeastern Cheboygan county, (T33N-R1W and T34N-R1W except a farm) were sold to the State for $8675.92 ($3.75 per acre) in June 1929.[36] Along M-32, about six miles east of Gaylord, KB sold its land with a deed restriction prohibiting cutting trees within 33 feet of the highway ditches, so there would always be trees shading the road.

In 1926, KB had expected to sell all its land in Montmorency County to a developer for a private club. They asked for $350,000, believing that it was worth a premium price because it was mostly in one block containing the Stock Farm and (Gaylanta) Lake 22. The price seemed high compared to other cutover land, but Lunden thought that the Salling Hanson Company's land could only be sold for $0.50 per acre because it was scattered, as well as sandy and infertile. Bigelow unrealistically insisted on a 50% down payment. Early in 1928, one real estate broker thought he had a group interested in buying all the KB and the Johannesburg Manufacturing Company land for $15 per acre. In reply to the broker's ebullient letter, Lunden wrote that it was more important to sell the land than to get $15 per acre. By December 1928, KB was happy to sell an option on all 22,966 acres of its land in Montmorency County—plus the farm equipment—for only $175,000, even allowing the payment to be spread over a three-year land contract. But the following month, the would-be buyer extended his option to April 15, 1929, and then allowed it to lapse. Negotiations continued, however.

Several factors during 1928 pushed KB[37] to sell its timberlands:

- First, in the spring, KB noticed declining sales. Notably, its lumber for making shoe heels was being undersold as much as $16 per thousand board-feet by heel stock from West Virginia and Pennsylvania. Additionally, KB's high grade maple lumber was being undersold by southern hardwoods.

- Second, the KB sawmill boilers were in very poor condition, might not last to saw all their timber, and would be expensive to replace.[38]

- Third, Bigelow was having great difficulty controlling his diabetes, and H. Lunden had had a heart attack, so both wanted to finish lumbering and shut down.

- Fourth, KB had been operating in a deflationary period of declining prices since 1924 that kept it from making money, so in 1928, H. Lunden compared business conditions with those of the Panic of 1896.[39]

- Fifth, real estate taxes were so high that holding the land to grow timber would have been unprofitable.

- Sixth, Bigelow wrote, "General overhead is altogether too much per thousand....Since 1920 there has been a steady decrease in the value of logs, which no one could help. With the volume of business declining because logging operations are tapering off, with no opportunity to buy logs and make a profit on it, the overhead on our operations is bound to increase, so it is going to eat up our principal [capital]. Consequently, the best thing to do is sell our holdings and realize all we can as quickly as we can."[40]

In other correspondence, Bigelow had explained that to conserve principal, the company must run at full speed until its timber was gone, then shut down as quickly as possible and liquidate assets. It was essential to sell the land quickly because there would be no income to pay real estate taxes after the last lumber had been sold. If, instead, the land sale took several years, it would be necessary to pay taxes from proceeds of land sales and the company would be liquidated with little return of capital to stockholders. That was what happened eventually.

The process of selling land was not easy, as one example shows. Among the timber lands KLB purchased from the David Ward Estate in 1912 were 1280 acres in southwestern Otsego County, T30N-R4W. This tract was too far away for KB to log it from the nearest camp (in T29N-R4W) but was too small to allow recovering the expense of building a new camp. Ross and Wentworth (R&W) owned adjoining timber land divided by KB's holding, so in the fall of 1927, Bigelow contacted R&W about buying its tract. Wentworth wanted to sell, but Ross did not, so they quoted a price of $263 per acre, too high by about $100. In September 1927, Bigelow wrote J. C. Holt, President of Antrim Iron (AI), that KB was interested in purchasing its 4600 acres of timber land in T30 & 31N-R4W. Holt replied that AI would be willing to sell its timber at $250 per acre. Bigelow responded that KB also would like to sell its timber at that price. Holt replied that he did not want to buy at that price, thus ending negotiations. Bigelow then offered the KB timber to other possible buyers, including R&W, Frank B. Ward, East Jordan Lumber, Kerry and Hanson Flooring Company, and others.

Early in these negotiations another problem surfaced. AI started to clear a path across the KB land for a railroad, believing that the Michigan Central Railroad (MCRR) had a railroad easement across the property. Lunden discovered that while there was such an easement in Charlevoix County, there was none in Otsego County, and furthermore, there was no easement on KB's deed from the Ward Estate. Bigelow told Lunden to stop AI building on KB property immediately, because KB wanted to sell the property and the buyer might object to the railroad. Lunden probably foresaw conflict arising on this, wished to distance himself from it, and break the news in a way to minimize animosity, because he might need to cross AI land in the future. He told Bigelow that he would give notice to AI to stop work, but Bigelow himself must deal with AI after that. Unfortunately, the AI manager, Mr. Durrett, was not in his office when Lunden gave the notice, but angrily phoned Lunden at eleven o'clock that night.

Eventually, Durrett persuaded R&W to buy KB's timberland and share the railroad with AI. An independent timber estimator appraised the timber before closing. This sale, closed in January 1929, left R&W with a 2040 acre tract, mostly in sections 19, 20, and 30, and cleared the way for KB to finish all its Lower Peninsula logging by the end of March 1929. Lunden said it was the best timber KB ever had, but because the company had to finish, it had to sell. The final price of $190,000 ($148 per acre) left KB little return for interest and taxes paid during its years of ownership. KB also agreed to buy, at set prices, R&W's output of flooring lumber for six months, approximately 2,000,000 board-feet. Apparently, R&W had been waiting for someone else to build the railroad before cutting its timber, because it had Percy Moots, who bought some of KB's equipment for the job, start logging the tract immediately.

Upper Peninsula Operations

Logging in the UP was less profitable than in the Lower Peninsula for many reasons.[41] Hauling logs was difficult because some of the soil was clay or muck that stayed wet and slippery, and the terrain was alternating swamp and ridges. Trees in the Lower Peninsula often produced three sixteen-foot logs before reaching the eight-inch top diameter limit, but in the UP a tree usually contained no more than one-sixteen foot and one-eight foot log. In some UP areas the maple wood was "sap stained" on the south side so it could only be used for railroad ties. The UP camps seemed to need more than their share of management attention for reasons discussed below.

Because only the best maple and hemlock logs could be shipped profitably 240 miles from the UP to Bay City, KB set up a leased portable sawmill at Camp 20, about five miles south of Soo Junction, to saw ties and timbers. As a consequence, the Bay City mills got fewer logs than expected from the UP and KB had to sell much of the Camp 20 output in unfamiliar UP markets. KB sold slabs from the sawmill for chemical wood. In 1928, KB purchased the portable sawmill and upgraded it in preparation for a big winter of production in 1928-29.

During the late summer of 1927, KB crews built five miles of railroad grade and track through its UP timber, making a new total of nine miles. When fall rains developed soft spots in the grade, more sand had to be hauled and the track raised from mud. Because the Soo Line Railroad would not go onto logging spurs to pick up cars of logs, KB had to buy a locomotive. After two months of shopping, in October 1927, KB bought a recently overhauled small Mogul locomotive from the Detroit and Mackinac Railway and had it relabeled "Kneeland-Bigelow No. 1". In January 1928, the company bought three standard gauge Russell logging cars from the Duluth Iron and Metal Company to haul logs to the portable sawmill. Russell cars were much simplified railroad cars with no floors or walls. Instead, they had two crosswise wooden beams about eight feet long (called bunks) for the logs to lie on lengthwise of the car.[42] The logs were held on the cars by a chain and spur at each end of the bunks, so the logs could be allowed to roll off the car by unfastening the chains with a pike or peavey. This was more convenient than having stakes at the ends of the bunks. Russell cars were usually made from kits of metal parts supplied by the Russell Wheel and Foundry Company in Detroit, plus wooden beams produced near where the cars themselves were assembled.

Camp 20 was larger than the other KB camps and actually included two camps located in the Sage River basin from three to eight miles south of Soo Junction. Its inventory for December 1928 covered seventeen typed legal-sized pages. Camp 20 employed substantially more men than any other KB camp during 1927 to 1929. Many were piece-rate workers with families, so the company store had a large retail business. In 1924, Lunden wrote to the Mackinac County School Commissioner insisting that a school be provided for the children of families working for KB near Hendrick's Corner.

On October 28, 1926, Lester Lunden listed what KB had removed from approximately 880 acres in the UP: 4,235,030 logs, 32,653 ties, 25,739 posts, 2680 cords of bark, 412 cords of balsam pulpwood, 482 cords of spruce pulpwood, and 326 poles. By September 30, 1928, KB had cut 12,260,790 board-feet from Camp 20, only about 29% of the saw timber estimated to be there when the land was purchased. Now, Herman Lunden was debating with Bigelow about selling the tract because they were not making money there.

Lunden opposed the sale, responding to Bigelow:[43]

- The corporate overhead charges of $3.31 per thousand board-feet for officers' salaries were what made the operation unprofitable, while the officers did nothing useful for the woods operation. (Because KB logged with directly employed crews, overhead charges applied to logging operations.)
- KB's accounting system charged all overhead to logging operations, whereas 50% should have been charged to swamp timber and ties sold.
- With the railroad and new camps built, and the portable sawmill refurbished, the big expenses had been covered.
- The price of lumber was going down, and no one wanted to buy the UP standing timber, so the best way to get the company's money out was to cut the

timber and sell the products.
- If Camp 20 were shut down, no men would be there to protect the timber from fire.

Despite Lunden's arguments, the company decided to sell the tract. Louis Smith cruised it during May through July 1928 to estimate the timber still uncut, omitting what would be cut during the winter of 1928-9. The cruise showed 30,881,000 board-feet left, a close correlation with 29,625,000 calculated from cutting records and the original estimates by Smith. Unfortunately, standing timber now was valued at only $4.00 to $6.00 per thousand board-feet, depending on species, instead of the $7.19 paid for it in more prosperous times. Similarly, railroad ties, cedar poles and pulpwood valued at $43,955, and remaining saw timber worth $150,849 had a combined value of $194,804, well below the book cost of $218,790 for the saw timber alone. Clearly, the apparent value of the asset had decreased. KB also had invested $35,325 in camps and railroad. The company valued the land without timber at $42,185.

Bigelow offered the timber to at least eight companies. When offered the tract, Mr. Bushong of Northwestern Cooperage and Lumber in Gladstone wrote to Bigelow, "Are not interested in buying KB property in T45N-7W & 8W because we have been operating in that territory without profit for twelve years and believe it best to get out. There is a large percentage of hemlock, out of which it is impossible to make any money." On June 10, 1929 a buyer took an option to buy for $275,000 but let it drop. The UP camps were put on a caretaker basis in the summer of 1929 after the cut timber had been shipped out. KB left the standing timber until it could be sold. The Chippewa county land was sold in 1936 for a book profit of $581. KB booked a profit of $70,730 on sale of the Luce County timber in 1937 and retained the land until it could be sold.

PANORAMIC VIEW OF THE WATER STREET LUMBER YARD AND SAW MILL OF THE KNEELAND-BIGELOW COMPANY.

BAY CITY, MICH. THIS PLANT RUNS DAY AND NIGHT THROUGHOUT THE YEAR, CUTTING NORTHERN HARDWOODS AND HEMLOCK.

Part II

THE COMPANY OPERATING METHODS

The Mills in Bay City

Instead of setting up a mill in the area of logging, as M&H had done, KB bought an existing Bay City sawmill in 1901. The first KB sawmill was called the Water Street Mill or Plant 1. It was on thirty acres located between 19th and 21st Streets, between South Water Street and the east bank of the Saginaw River. Maps in 1879 and 1891 show this had been the Rust and Company sawmill and that other sawmills occupied the space KB used later for storing lumber.[44] This mill had only a single band saw with a capacity of 120,000 board-feet (bd-ft) per shift and no finishing capability. Band saws and their equipment were more expensive than circular saws, but they had the advantage of being only half as thick, so they wasted less of the logs in sawdust, an important concern to KB. Large circular saws would weave as they cut, so the boards would not be uniform in thickness. Band saws did not weave, and so cut boards uniformly. An edger saw was used to square each board, give it a standard width, and in the process remove the bark with the edges. After adding a resaw, KB started running the mill in October 1901. (A resaw made narrower boards from wide ones, as for flooring.)

Bigelow had expected the mill to saw 18 to 20 million board feet per year, but its production was usually lower.[45] In 1904, the mill employed eighty men. During repairs in August 1926, the maximum log length the Water Street Mill could use was shortened to 26 feet from 44 feet.[46] The capability of sawing very long boards had given the mill this special business, an advantage the M&H sawmill in Lewiston also enjoyed. Some elm logs too big in diameter for the sawmill were split with dynamite while in the woods.

Photos by John D. Cress

Log train on Water Street, with cart load of firewood, 1910.

Water Street sawmill from the Saginaw River, 1910.

The mill yard could store 7,000,000 to 8,000,000 bd-ft of lumber plus 300,000 bd-ft of logs in its pond. R. G. Baker was the Water Street mill superintendent during the late 1920's. The mill finished its cut on April 17, 1929, then was dismantled.

Sawmills had to be located where a log storage boom could be created on a river or pond. If at a curve in the river, the mill had to be on the slow water side. Storing logs in water prevented their cracking or being eaten by worms during summer storage[47] and allowed dirt to fall off. If logs were sawed while frozen, the edges of the boards were apt to crack and downgrade the product. Storing in the hot pond (kept unfrozen with steam from the mill) thawed frozen logs. Mills on the Saginaw River did not use a boom of floating logs chained together to hold the logs in place because the boom logs would become waterlogged in a couple of years and have to be replaced. Also, if the log boom on a river broke, the logs quickly would be carried downstream and scattered. Instead, two short jetties extending into the river at right angles to its current formed the log storage ponds at this mill. A short distance beyond the ends of these jetties, a long jetty extended upstream parallel to the river current. This kept some river water flowing through the ponds and protected them from river boat traffic.[44] (See sketch following.)

Water Street sawmill from the brewery showing Saginaw River, 1910.

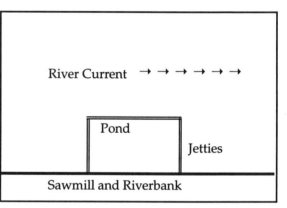

Freshly cut lumber had to be allowed to air dry four to twelve weeks before it was ready to use or to go through a planing mill. "Stringers" were placed on the ground at right angles to the boards, and arranged to give the piled boards some slope. Other stringers were added at four-foot intervals between each layer of boards. The top of the pile was protected from rain by a "cap" of 1-by-12 inch boards resting on two-inch thick boards on edge, four feet apart, each board gaining two inches of width going toward the high side of the pile.[48] Fresh piles were as high above the tramways as a man could reach to make maximum use of the ground space.

John D. Cress in a 1910 article in American Lumberman[49] described the KB sawmills as follows:

Lumber pile at the Belinda Street sawmill, 1910.

The yards are kept strictly clean and no rubbish or waste lumber is permitted to accumulate around either plant. No refuse burner is employed at either mill, all waste wood that is not needed for the boilers being sold for firewood. The company employs several teams in delivering wood in Bay City and Saginaw and ships a considerable quantity to outside points. This is one of many indications of a policy of conservation which characterizes all branches of the business. Waste is guarded against wherever possible. As an illustration of this fact, the company cuts odd lengths wherever it can effect a saving by so doing.

In August 1927, a truck replaced the horses used to deliver firewood in Bay City, and they were sent to Camps 20 and 22.

The sawmill located beside the Saginaw River between Sherman and Belinda Streets was known as the Belinda Street Mill, the KLB Mill, or Plant 2. The mill was purchased from Wylie-Buell and earlier known as the Detroit Mill. Although Wylie-Buell and KBB were completely separate companies, the mill sawed logs from Wylie-Buell, while KBB sold logs and hemlock bark to Wylie-Buell. The mill had a double-band saw and a fifty-acre site extending almost to the Belinda Street Bridge. Normal stock at the Belinda Street Mill was 10,000,000 bd-ft, along with 800,000 bd-ft of logs in its ponds. Fire destroyed the mill on June 12, 1925, and it was not rebuilt. KB replaced its production capacity by contracting with the Island Lumber Company (located on an island called the Middle Ground and also known as Watson & Richardson) for sawing at $6 per thousand board-feet for hardwood and $5 for softwoods. To fulfill this contract, Island put on a night shift at its sawmill until 1928.

The newspaper report of the Belinda Street Mill fire says:[50]

The mill . . . a landmark in Bay City, one of the largest sawmills in the State . . . having been rebuilt and enlarged considerably . . . thoroughly modern, and was in operation until 5:30 in the afternoon . . . fire . . . started after 9:30 . . . that night. Spontan-eous combustion is the only cause so far blamed for

Belinda Street sawmill timber storage dock, 1910.

Belinda Street sawmill showing waste wood chutes (called pockets) loading a cart with firewood, whereas sawmills usually have a waste burner. The spark arrestor on the chimney and a sheet metal roof prevented fires. The cupola was for both ventillation and light. 1910.

the fire, which throws more than 80 men out of employment. Mr. Wrape said, . . . every precaution was taken to guard against [spontaneous combustion] and all dust in the mill was cleaned up every night . . . high wind carried the burning embers across the river and started numerous fires on the west side . . . No less than 25 different fires started at the plant of the Bradley-Miller Company, all of which were extinguished without material damage.

Photos by John D. Cress

KB office building with Charles Bigelow and Walter Wrape on porch, 1910.

Fire fighters kept the fire from spreading to the piles of lumber outside the mill and to adjacent buildings. Fine sawdust in a mill can catch fire spontaneously, so careful, thorough, and frequent cleanup is a necessary safety measure, although sawmill fires were frequent.

After the fire, KB sent a log loader and crew from the camps to help move logs from Belinda Street to the Water Street Mill. As a sign of changing times, the crew members preferred to drive their own cars rather than accompany the loader on the train. The eight or nine teams of horses that had been delivering waste wood from the sawmill for sale in Bay City were sent to Camp 8. Logs in the river boom were towed to the Water Street Mill.

It appears that Plant 3 was at 800 Marquette Street in Bay City, although KB also owned another tract on Marquette at Sidman. It had twenty-three drying kilns, and a flooring mill with five planer and matcher units for a total capacity of more than 50,000 bd-ft per day, making KB one of the largest producers of hardwood flooring in the world.[51] Planers smoothed the top and bottom surfaces while matchers made tongue and groove cuts in the side and end surfaces. The flooring was sold under the brand names "B-C-Co", "Electric", "Bigelow", and after Pierson Kneeland took over management, "Knone Better". The mill superintendent in 1925 was William E. Sims. Although Bigelow believed KB made $5 per thousand board-feet by having the flooring mill,[52] apparently it was not very profitable. A salt well on the property was one of the last two operated in the Bay City area.[53] Producing salt was typical for Bay City mills, which used left-over steam to

dry the salt. The planing mill, storage for lumber, and company office in the 1930's were all at 800 Marquette Street.

KB manufactured hardwood flooring that was in the form of boards with standard widths of 1-1/2, 2, 2-1/4, and 3-1/4 inches. The boards were narrow so if they warped, it would not be noticeable. Standard lengths up to sixteen feet were available, but for Number 1 grade, there were up to 40% random lengths of 1-1/2 to 3-1/2 feet, cut to a length that eliminated defects. There were four grades: Clear, Number 1, Number 2, and Factory. Standard thicknesseswere 3/8, 25/32, and 33/32 inches. The boards were tongue and groove matched on both sides and ends. When floors were laid, the boards were forced together so there was no space showing between boards. To achieve this, the boards had to be kiln dried for several days to remove all moisture before milling and then kept dry. Machinery for milling the boards had to be kept accurate to make the boards fit together properly. The boards were installed parallel to room walls on subflooring that had been laid diagonally. The boards were fastened to the subflooring by nails with conical heads, somewhat like finishing nails, driven slightly off vertical into a nail head groove near the base of the tongue, so there would be no space between the boards and no nails showed on the finished floor. KB's advertising brochure[50] described flooring and its grades but did not mention parquet flooring, although its advertising blotter (photo) boasted: "If it's flooring—we make it."

The mills' output was sold mostly in Michigan and Ohio, but some flooring and heel stock (lumber used for making heels of women's shoes) went to the Atlantic coast and Europe. In 1909, KB mills cut 50% hemlock. In 1911, their two sawmills manufactured 23,000,000 board-feet, which was fifteen percent of a total 153,458,176 board-feet of hemlock manufactured in eastern Michigan.[54] This high percentage of hemlock did not continue during the 1920s. During KB ownership, the mills cut a total of 685,000,000 board-feet of all species of lumber. The largest amount cut in any one year (1911) was approximately 42,000,000 board-feet, and diminished gradually thereafter.[55] KB sold much of its lumber to the automobile industry

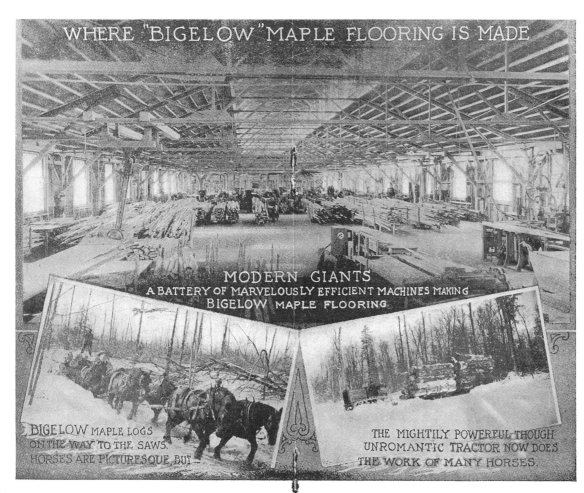

Flooring mill inside, ca. 1926, KB advertising brochure.

Former Marquette Street flooring or planing mill, 1989.

Ink blotter showing details of KB flooring, 1936.

for use in automobile frames, wheels, and crates for parts, and to the furniture industry and retail lumber yards. Probably, lumber was sold to the large wagon and carriage manufacturing industry that preceded the automotive industry in Michigan as well. Walter Wrape was the salesman until he became secretary-treasurer and Albert Blixberg replaced him, traveling the Great Lakes states.

Sawmill productivity has increased significantly during the twentieth century. In 1983, the newer of the Pinkham Mills in Maine could produce 31,250 board-feet per hour with 36 men on a shift. By contrast, the double-band saw

Belinda Street mill in 1907 averaged only 6972 board-feet per hour with 80 men on a shift.

To place KB's production in a larger perspective, it should be noted that in 1920, nineteen Michigan mills cut more than 10,000,000 board-feet, and a total of 726,147,000 was cut by all mills in the state. Michigan was the country's leading producer of maple lumber with 36.4% of the U.S. total.[57] By October 1926, production had decreased so Lunden wrote that no large sawmill remained along the Detroit and Mackinac Railway between Cheboygan and Bay City.[58]

KB and Predecessor Companies Annual Lumber Production (In Board-Feet) by Mill[56]

Year	Water Street	Island Lbr. & Belinda Street	Total Sawed	Lumber + Flooring
1907		20,112,280		
1910 Nov.		1,758,337		
1911 Nov.	1,539,660	2,088,975	42,000,000 (all year)	
1912 Mar.	1,507,962	1,574,882		
*1917	18,795,232	13,613,601	32,408,833	
1918	12,048,268	9,811,212	21,859,480	
1919	12,425,096	9,535,956	21,961,052	
1920	8,823,393	9,990,873	18,814,266	
1921	5,039,256	7,338,992	12,378,248	
1922				42,622,876
1923			17,499,695	40,248,614
1924	6,878,790	11,540,395	18,419,185	28,204,936
1925	13,936,219	6,273,368	20,209,587	27,395,148
1926xDec.	12,553,638	5,581,769	18.405,407	23,735,109
1927	14.348,345	1,626,797	15,975,142	
1928	14,136,015	769,073	14,905,088	

*1913 - 1916 are not available

Logging and Cutting Operations

As a hardwood lumber manufacturing company, KB specialized in maple, birch and beech for flooring, although its ornately beautiful letterhead in 1913 mentioned pine, hemlock, and hardwood. In 1904, the company estimated that 40% of its standing timber near Lewiston was hemlock.[59] Unlike nineteenth-century pine lumbermen, KB had to cut for any products it could sell: railroad ties, mine props, piling, posts and poles of all sizes, trap net stakes, Excelsior bolts, box bolts. KB made cedar into shingles and blocks for foundations. Cedar, jack pine, and tamarack went to make water pipe. (The Michigan Pipe Company in Bay City had a letterhead showing a piece of pipe made of wood segments bound together with metal bands.) Black ash was sold for barrel hoops, ash and elm logs for barrel headings, birch for spools and clothespins. KB cut hemlock trees for lumber, railroad crossing planks, and bark to make tannic acid. Spruce and balsam were cut into pulpwood for paper; even jack pine cordwood was cut. White pine occurred in many KB hardwood stands and was the same age as the hardwood.[60] In my part of Section 23, there are still six or eight big pine stumps within a 200 foot radius where most other trees are hardwood. Bird's-eye maple trees could be identified by pits scattered along the tops of veins of bark, so the logs sometimes were handled separately and sold directly to a furniture manufacturer (at $100 per thousand board-feet). Products like pulpwood, posts, and bark that did not need to go to the mills in Bay City went directly from the woods to the customer.

Lunden had advised that certain stands of timber were immature and increasing their board-feet per acre and so should be left to be cut later, while others were mature and should be cut soon.[61] When he lumbered the more mature stand (at new Camp 2), he noticed an undue number of hollow stumps, indicating the trees should have been cut sooner. In another letter, he reported handling all diameters of logs because they were cutting hardwood not pine.[62] This indicates that trees in any one virgin hardwood forest were of all different ages, but trees in any one pine forest cut many

years ago were of the same age, just as forestry texts state now.

To get started in June 1901, KB had to hire men and buy equipment ranging from axes to a steam log loader.[63] Bigelow did the buying, spending most of the summer in Detroit. George Cross attended to hiring men, building a camp, and making more than two miles of railroad grade ready for the railroad crew to lay track.

A logging operation began with choosing the camp site. Locations among hemlock trees were avoided because they harbored bedbugs. There had to be a "tote road" to bring in supplies by truck, wagon or sleigh. After consultation with the railroad, there came surveying and profiling railroad spurs. (The profiles showed the depth and length of cuts and fills.) KB ordinarily built the railroad grades, but "gandy dancers" employed by the railroad usually laid tracks. When the railroad neared completion, construction of buildings began near the railroad on a level area with space for the "banking" ground (so named because originally it was on the bank of a river) where logs were "decked", that is, piled awaiting shipment. Loggers tried to minimize the space used for log decks to avoid the expense of clearing an area of stumps with dynamite. Next, they built wheel and sleigh roads from the banking grounds into the timber. No one liked building roads or railroad grades because it was steadily hard work. Road builders cut the timber that stood in the roadway and blasted out the stumps. "Dynamite Mike" could take out a stump and leave it lying at the side of the road with one blast.[64] The builders also leveled "cradle knolls" and filled hollows with horse drawn "slush scrapers" to make the road level from side to side and reduce its slope. Sleighs could not tolerate much slope sidewise although they could go up and downhill. Finally, a horse-drawn four-wheeled road grader smoothed the roads.

After logging preparations were completed, sawyers felled trees, and cut them to specified length for sawlogs. Sawyers had to fell trees skillfully, so they would not hang up in another tree and would fall where they could easily be hauled away. Swampers followed, cutting and clearing brush for narrow skid-roads used by skidders or teamsters to drag the logs out to a

Road grader drawn by four horses, ca.1920.

Notching a tree for cutting, New Camp 2, 1925.

Cutting the tree into log lengths, 1925.

Sawyers cutting a tree, 1925.

Skidding logs, New Camp 2, 1925.

Bunching the logs for hauling, 1925.

Log truck being loaded with an A-Jammer. Herman Lunden is second from left. Demonstration tractor is behind him, about 1915.

Photo by John D. Cress

Two teams on pole road near Camp 9. One car loaded with maple logs. Chas. Turner and Joe Donnelly on logs, 1910.

logging road and bunch them. On snow, a skidder could drag logs fairly easily, moving them far enough to make large piles for an A-jammer (an A-frame log loader) to work efficiently in loading a sleigh. When there was no snow, logging wheels supplemented the skidder by moving "bunches" of logs to a jammer, or even all the way to the deck (log pile) alongside the railroad. Because logging wheels required a road almost twice as wide as the big wagons called "trucks", (see photo) they rarely were used to haul logs farther than a quarter mile. Trucks had a different disadvantage: They had to be loaded from bunches with jammers that required time to move and setup.

Log trucks were strongly built wagons without floors, and not what we now think of as trucks, although that name was commonly applied to wagons without a box early in this century. Very similar wagons ran on "pole roads" that resembled railroads but used wooden poles in place of steel rails. Pole road cars (see photo) used steel wheels with concave rims to

stay on the poles. Pole road cars could carry very heavy loads because the poles distributed the weight over a large area, but required a fairly level path so they would not coast and get out of control. There do not appear to be brakes on pole cars and the teamster was not in a position to operate brakes. For example, three pole roads ran up ravines west of Camp 6 and also were used in other camps where there was level ground. During the 1920s, KB did not use pole roads; perhaps their log trucks (wagons) with wide rimmed wheels sufficed or they used more spur railroads if there was space to pile logs alongside. Pole road car wheels do not appear in Marshall-Wells 1928 catalog, so they must have gone out of general use by that time.

Whenever possible, loggers wanted to load logs onto cars without first decking them (called "hot logging"). Clearly, the foreman had to make some complicated decisions about how the logs should be handled, knowing his costs would be compared with costs of other foremen. Kneeland-McLurg and others working on less hilly terrain built very rough logging railroads instead of wheel and sleigh roads.[65] Lunden found road building in May cheapest because by then the ground had dried out but was still soft, and the weather was still cool enough so men and horses could work harder than in summer.[66]

Generally, lumberjacks did whatever work was needed at the time, regardless of their particular skills; they were lumbering jacks of all trades. Some men with special skills, such as toploaders, would leave a camp if their skill was not needed.[67] When the logs were out of the woods, the lumberjacks went elsewhere because they considered it beneath them to cut cordwood from the tops and leftover hardwood trees not usable for logs. Companies such as Michigan Iron & Chemical Company or the Antrim Iron Company recruited men in Kentucky to cut the residue into cordwood for making chemicals. The cordwood was hauled to kilns at the chemical company's plant, then heated to drive out acetone, wood alcohol, and other chemicals for distillation, leaving charcoal that the chemical companies used to reduce iron ore to pig iron. The woodcutters, who cut after logging was completed, were usually family men and lived with their families in a row of small buildings in the "wood camp". Wood camps differed from logging camps in several other ways: they had no cook camp because each family supplied its own food; they had a barn for the horses, but the teamsters had to buy feed for their horses; and work was paid for on a piece-rate basis. Small jobbers for logs and swamp timber operated in about the same way as woodcutter camps.

Horses always formed the backbone of KB's log hauling to the railroad, and provided the cheapest and easiest means of skidding logs. Intelligent workers, horses stopped if a log became caught, and looked around to see what their teamster wanted done. Abuse of KB horses quickly got a man into trouble. Men liked being teamsters because they liked horses and/or liked controlling these large animals, doing things an unassisted man could not do, and it was easier than other woods work. KB still bought horses in 1925, and used six to eight carloads of oats per year to feed them. Horses could work in deeper snow, and so were preferred to oxen, the other animals widely used in logging.[68] Oxen were fitted with yokes, and therefore lacked harness with a breeching strap behind their thighs that would give them the means to brake loads. Normally, they only skid-

Sprinkler sleigh at loading tank, ca. 1920.

ded logs and pulled "pungs" (drays or stone boats); they seldom pulled log trucks and never sleighs. In both summer and winter, working oxen wore a clever plate designed to fit each side of their cloven hoof.

Winter log hauling operations depended on crawler tractors with special treads and horses having shoes with calks working on well-iced roads that were as smooth as new pavement.[69] Horse drawn sprinklers built up the ice by operating in the coldest hours of the night, so the water froze quickly before it could run off the road. The simply-built sprinkler consisted of a rectangular wooden box tank mounted on a sleigh equipped with torches at its corners to help the driver see. (see photo) Tongues at both ends allowed it to be pulled in either direction because they might run out of water where there was no space to turn around. (A tongue is a pole about 15 feet long fastened to the harness between a team of two horses and fastened to the front sleigh or wheels to steer them in the direction the horses are going.)

Ice roads would be seriously damaged if used when the temperature was above freezing, so often log hauling started at 2:00 a.m., requiring the cooks to prepare an extra meal. For rush situations, log hauling might be done around the clock in two twelve-hour shifts. Snow, reflecting light from clear winter skies, usually provided adequate illumination for night work. If not, haulers used trail marker lanterns (small kerosene burning flares). The ice roads had to be kept clear of debris and manure by a man whose job title was "chickadee."

KB used horse drawn sleighs with "bunks" nine feet wide (twelve feet with tractors) so sleighs could carry 4000 bd-ft of logs in one load for distances up to four miles. As many as seven tiers of logs could be loaded on a sleigh. Unloaded sleighs traveled with bunks turned parallel to the runners, so there would be more space for meeting an oncoming sleigh. Sleighs outnumbered teams and teamsters, so they did not need to wait for sleighs to be loaded or unloaded. Steep downhill slopes were sanded to slow the sleighs and keep them from running into the horses. Sanding was Dynamite Mike's winter job. At Camp 23, he took revenge on teamsters by leaving a downhill unsanded, forc-

ing the horses to hold back the load. When the horses could no longer hold the load, they ran to keep ahead, at the risk of accident. An incautious driver could upend his tractor while trying to start a sleigh frozen to icy ground.[70] To prevent the runners freezing to the ice during loading and unloading, sleighs stopped on a small pole.

There were signicant disadvantages to operating during summertime. Once decked on the banking ground beside the railroad, logs could be shipped to the mill when needed, but getting them into a pond by summertime was desirable to prevent cracking, or, for pine, worm damage. Activity in the woods diminished during summer because log hauling costs rose, fewer men were available because of employment in farming and construction, and accumulated logs soon suffered damage. When KB was cutting hardwood timber, its crews worked on clay and soils that do not dry out as quickly as pine growing soils. Rainy weather and heavily-laden steel-tired wheels quickly churned deep mud that slowed operations and raised costs, so there was a significant advantage to operating during winter when the ground was frozen and ice roads could be used. Additonally, swamp timber was only accessible when the ground was frozen.

A portable shingle mill operated by a jobber was associated with KB's Lower Peninsula logging operation. It was located close to the cedar cutting because lots of waste was produced and had to be disposed of. One location was three miles northwest of Atlanta on the BCG&ARR west of Green's Crossing. (Another company's mill was at the Shingle Mill bridge on the Black River.) The shingles were sawed, not cut with a knife.[71] The shingle mill's capacity was 15,000 to 18,000 shingles per day.

Hemlock cutting and bark peeling had a specialized practice. It had to be cut after freezing temperatures arrived in the late fall and peeled after warm weather returned in the spring. As a result, hemlock logs could only be sent to the mill in spring and early summer. Men removed the bark from hemlock logs with a tool called a bark spud. (It was a bit like a long handled shovel except it had a flat blade only four inches wide.) A very similar tool is used now to plant

Sleigh loaded with logs, New Camp 3 at Hallock, 1922.

Five cars loaded and log decks near Camp 10. About 800,000 bd-ft. in sight, mainly maple with some beech and elm, 1910.

Photo by John D. Cress

Decks of hemlock logs and Camp 6, northeast of Lewiston, 1910.

seedling trees. Eight to ten percent of hemlock logs would not peel, but still could be sawed into lumber.

Lower Peninsula hemlock bark contained 11% to 14% tannic acid, while UP and northern Wisconsin bark had less tannic acid content.[72] Hemlock bark sales shrank in the late 1920s as tanners began using "extract"; however, KB sold 600 to 800 cords of bark in the spring of 1929 to Tanner's Supply Company in Grand Rapids and to Michigan Pole and Tie Company in Newberry. Like other products that did not have to go to the mills in Bay City, bark was shipped directly to the customer. Carpenters disliked using hemlock lumber because it had

slivers, was brittle, split easily, and could not be planed or finished as well as pine. Railroad managements considered it too soft for ties, but used it for grade crossing planks. It was much cheaper than pine for lumbermen to produce because much of the cost of cutting could be apportioned to the valuable bark.

Hardwood ties needed a preservative treatment. Cedar ties did not need preservative, but were too soft to stand the traffic of main line use. By the late 1920s, the MCRR bought only hardwood ties although other railroads still bought some softwood ties. KB shipped a total of 150,000 ties cut along the Davidson branch of the MCRR.

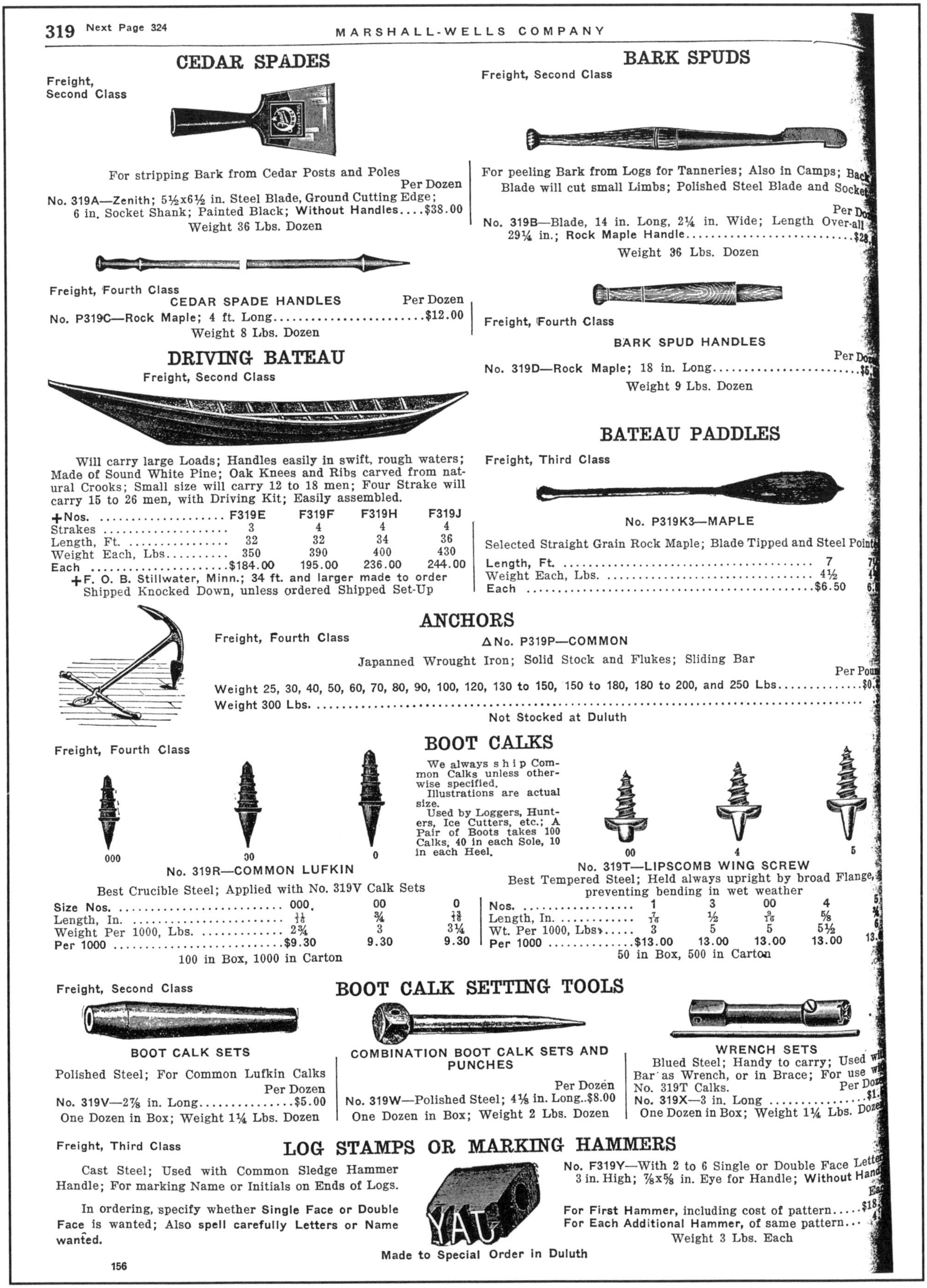

319 Next Page 324 MARSHALL-WELLS COMPANY

CEDAR SPADES

Freight, Second Class

For stripping Bark from Cedar Posts and Poles

Per Dozen

No. 319A—Zenith; 5½x6½ in. Steel Blade, Ground Cutting Edge; 6 in. Socket Shank; Painted Black; Without Handles....$38.00

Weight 36 Lbs. Dozen

Freight, Fourth Class

CEDAR SPADE HANDLES Per Dozen

No. P319C—Rock Maple; 4 ft. Long........................$12.00

Weight 8 Lbs. Dozen

DRIVING BATEAU

Freight, Second Class

Will carry large Loads; Handles easily in swift, rough waters; Made of Sound White Pine; Oak Knees and Ribs carved from natural Crooks; Small size will carry 12 to 18 men; Four Strake will carry 15 to 26 men, with Driving Kit; Easily assembled.

+Nos.	F319E	F319F	F319H	F319J
Strakes	3	4	4	4
Length, Ft.	32	32	34	36
Weight Each, Lbs.	350	390	400	430
Each	$184.00	195.00	236.00	244.00

+F. O. B. Stillwater, Minn.; 34 ft. and larger made to order

Shipped Knocked Down, unless ordered Shipped Set-Up

BARK SPUDS

Freight, Second Class

For peeling Bark from Logs for Tanneries; Also in Camps; Back Blade will cut small Limbs; Polished Steel Blade and Socket

Per Do

No. 319B—Blade, 14 in. Long, 2¼ in. Wide; Length Over-all 29¼ in.; Rock Maple Handle..........................$28.

Weight 36 Lbs. Dozen

Freight, Fourth Class

BARK SPUD HANDLES

Per Do

No. 319D—Rock Maple; 18 in. Long........................$5.

Weight 9 Lbs. Dozen

BATEAU PADDLES

Freight, Third Class

No. P319K3—MAPLE

Selected Straight Grain Rock Maple; Blade Tipped and Steel Point

Length, Ft.	7	7
Weight Each, Lbs.	4½	4
Each	$6.50	6.

ANCHORS

Freight, Fourth Class

ΔNo. P319P—COMMON

Japanned Wrought Iron; Solid Stock and Flukes; Sliding Bar

Per Pou

Weight 25, 30, 40, 50, 60, 70, 80, 90, 100, 120, 130 to 150, 150 to 180, 180 to 200, and 250 Lbs..............$0.

Weight 300 Lbs. ....

Not Stocked at Duluth

BOOT CALKS

Freight, Fourth Class

We always ship Common Calks unless otherwise specified.

Illustrations are actual size.

Used by Loggers, Hunters, Ice Cutters, etc.; A Pair of Boots takes 100 Calks, 40 in each Sole, 10 in each Heel.

000 00 0

No. 319R—COMMON LUFKIN

Best Crucible Steel; Applied with No. 319V Calk Sets

Size Nos.	000	00	0
Length, In.	11/16	¾	13/16
Weight Per 1000, Lbs.	2¾	3	3¼
Per 1000	$9.30	9.30	9.30

100 in Box, 1000 in Carton

00 4 5

No. 319T—LIPSCOMB WING SCREW

Best Tempered Steel; Held always upright by broad Flange, preventing bending in wet weather

Nos.	1	3	00	4	5
Length, In.	7/16	½	9/16	⅝	¾
Wt. Per 1000, Lbs.	3	5	5	5½	6
Per 1000	$13.00	13.00	13.00	13.00	13.

50 in Box, 500 in Carton

BOOT CALK SETTING TOOLS

Freight, Second Class

BOOT CALK SETS

Polished Steel; For Common Lufkin Calks

Per Dozen

No. 319V—2⅞ in. Long..............$5.00

One Dozen in Box; Weight 1¼ Lbs. Dozen

COMBINATION BOOT CALK SETS AND PUNCHES

Per Dozen

No. 319W—Polished Steel; 4⅛ in. Long..$8.00

One Dozen in Box; Weight 2 Lbs. Dozen

WRENCH SETS

Blued Steel; Handy to carry; Used with Bar as Wrench, or in Brace; For use with No. 319T Calks.

Per Doz

No. 319X—3 in. Long ....$1.

One Dozen in Box; Weight 1¼ Lbs. Dozen

LOG STAMPS OR MARKING HAMMERS

Freight, Third Class

Cast Steel; Used with Common Sledge Hammer Handle; For marking Name or Initials on Ends of Logs.

In ordering, specify whether Single Face or Double Face is wanted; Also spell carefully Letters or Name wanted.

No. F319Y—With 2 to 6 Single or Double Face Letters 3 in. High; ⅞x⅝ in. Eye for Handle; Without Handle

Each

For First Hammer, including cost of pattern.....$18.

For Each Additional Hammer, of same pattern...4

Weight 3 Lbs. Each

Made to Special Order in Duluth

156

Marshall-Wells 1928 catalog page showing bark spuds, boot calks, and marking hammers.

Logging Equipment

Ralph Clement Bryant described logging techniques of the early twentieth century in great detail in his textbook for foresters.[73] His book includes 48 pages defining terms used in logging, a necessity because the terms used in Michigan differed from those used elsewhere. The following descriptions came mostly from Fred White and Walter Thompson and reflected KB practice.

Before bulldozers, "slush" or "scoop" scrapers moved earth for road building and other construction.[74] The scraper, shaped like a kitchen scoop, was about 33 inches square and ten inches deep at its back. "Pipe" handles attached to each side stuck out behind 18 or 24 inches. A team of horses pulled the scraper by a chain attached to a steel yoke. The yoke attached to pivot pins near the tops of the sides of the scraper and about one foot from its front edge and had to be long enough to clear the back end of the scoop when dumping. Pulling the scraper yoke gave the force on the top of the scraper an effect like "power assistance" for the man controlling the scraper, allowing the handling of as much a third of a yard of earth. Lifting both handles at the same time made the front of the scraper dig in and pick up earth. Lifting just one handle made the opposite front corner dig in, tip over, and dump the scraper. One man drove the horses while the other operated the scraper. Some scrapers were mounted on wheels. (catalog page 436)

Properly sharpening a saw is very important for quick and easy tree cutting.[75] Sharpening a saw has two phases: "setting" and "filing". Setting consists of slightly bending the points of the teeth in alternate directions so the saw cut will be wider than the thickness of the saw to prevent binding. The amount of set required is in proportion to the amount of sap and pitch in the wood because these make the saw stick. Less set is required when the wood is frozen. Excessive set slows the cutting. To check whether the set is correct without actually using the saw, four set-gauges to match various conditions are used. The set-gauge, called a "spider", is steel and has three legs that stand on the saw blade, and a finger that just touches the tip of the saw tooth if the set is correct. When the set of a large crosscut saw must be increased or decreased, a saw-set tool is used. The tool is steel, seven inches long and three-fourths inch wide and thick. Its top has a flat surface for the saw blade, then a convex surface near one end to set the curvature of the saw tooth. The bottom of the saw set has two fingers to be hammered into a stump or board to hold the saw set steady. Then the saw can be laid on the saw set and each tooth hammered to bend it to the correct curvature.

The teeth of a large crosscut saw are arranged in pairs of triangular cutting teeth bent in opposite directions for set. Between each pair of cutting teeth is a raker tooth to pull the sawdust out of the saw cut. Until raker teeth were invented by Disston, saws could not make horizontal cuts as when cutting down a tree. Rakers have no set and must be kept filed a little shorter than the cutting teeth. Filing is done with a raker gauge, a steel tool 2.2 by 5 inches by 0.5 inch thick with two adjusting screws. The gauge is also used to hold a file moved over the cutting teeth to ensure that they are all the same length. When the cutting teeth are filed, one edge of all the teeth facing the filer is done at a time. The filer requires skill to hold the file to get the correct angle.

In small camps, sawyers filed their own saws, but a large logging camp employed a saw filer who worked indoors at a chest-high bench in front of a row of windows for lots of light. (The windows also gave a good view of the camp, so the filer supposedly knew everything going on.) On the filer's six-foot-long bench, two 2 by 4's were fastened about two inches apart. The saw was positioned between the 2 by 4's with two boards cut to match the curve of a saw and extending up to the teeth to support them while being filed. The boards and saw were fastened between the 2 by 4's with thin wedges between the holding boards and the saw. If there was no shop, the filer fastened his bench to a special sawhorse about four feet high.

Logs were "skidded" by a team of two horses from where they fell to a log loader. Skidding tongs attached the skidding chain to a log. They resembled the tongs used to carry ice blocks,

MARSHALL-WELLS COMPANY 436

SCRAPERS AND ROAD DRAGS

Freight. Third Class

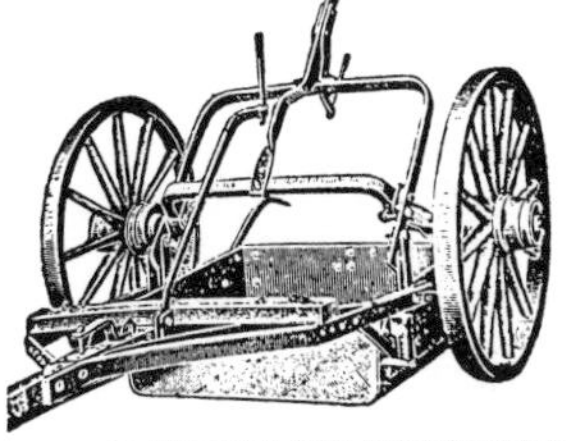

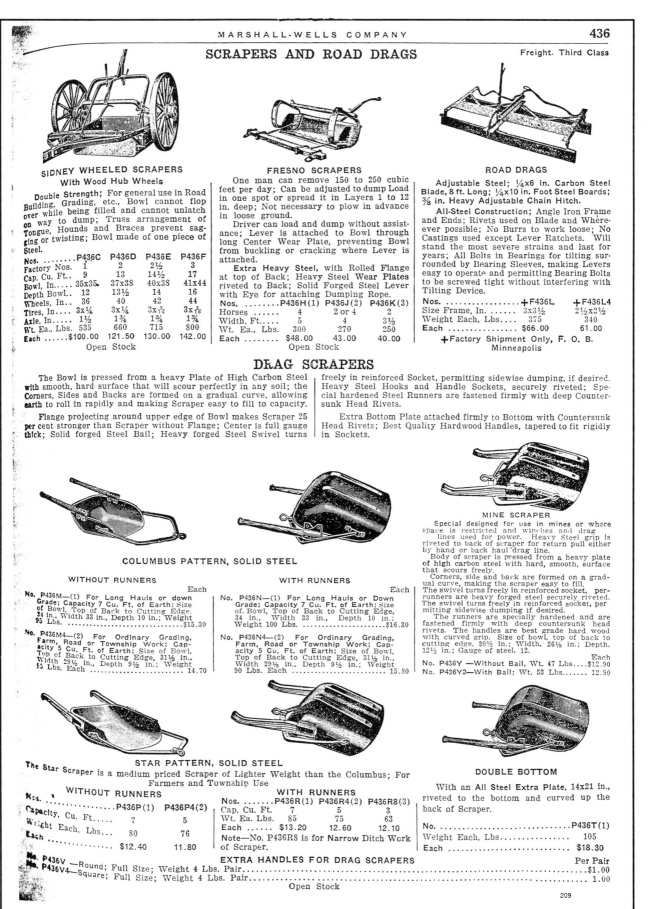

SIDNEY WHEELED SCRAPERS

With Wood Hub Wheels

Double Strength; For general use in Road Building, Grading, etc., Bowl cannot flop over while being filled and cannot unlatch on way to dump; Truss arrangement of Tongue, Hounds and Braces prevent sagging or twisting; Bowl made of one piece of Steel.

Nos.	P436C	P436D	P436E	P436F
Factory Nos.	1	2	2½	3
Cap. Cu. Ft..	9	13	14½	17
Bowl, In.....	35x35	37x38	40x38	41x44
Depth Bowl..	12	13½	14	16
Wheels, In..	36	40	42	44
Tires, In....	3x¼	3x¼	3x5/16	3x5/16
Axle, In.....	1½	1¾	1¾	1¾
Wt. Ea., Lbs.	535	660	715	800
Each	$100.00	121.50	130.00	142.00

Open Stock

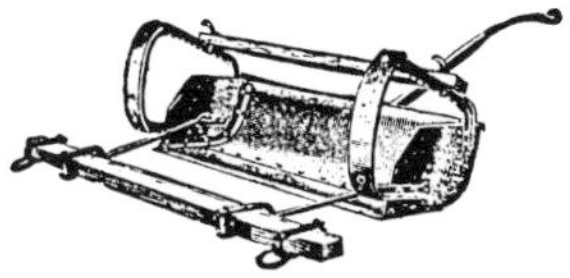

FRESNO SCRAPERS

One man can remove 150 to 250 cubic feet per day; Can be adjusted to dump Load in one spot or spread it in Layers 1 to 12 in. deep; Not necessary to plow in advance in loose ground.

Driver can load and dump without assistance; Lever is attached to Bowl through long Center Wear Plate, preventing Bowl from buckling or cracking where Lever is attached.

Extra Heavy Steel, with Rolled Flange at top of Back; **Heavy Steel Wear Plates** riveted to Back; Solid Forged Steel Lever with Eye for attaching Dumping Rope.

Nos.	P436H(1)	P436J(2)	P436K(3)
Horses	4	2 or 4	2
Width, Ft.....	5	4	3½
Wt. Ea., Lbs.	300	270	250
Each	$48.00	43.00	40.00

Open Stock

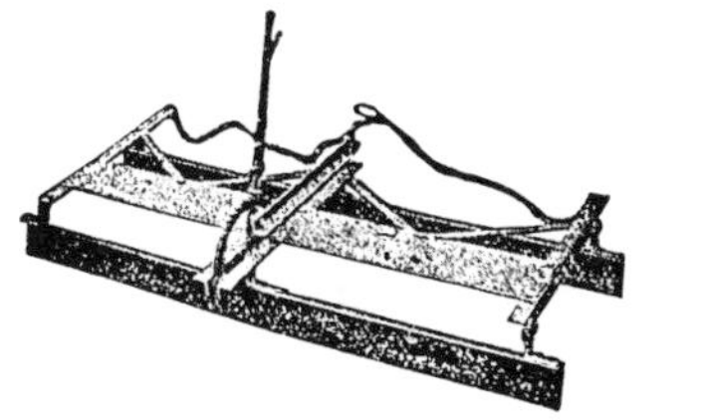

ROAD DRAGS

Adjustable Steel; ¼x6 in. Carbon Steel Blade, 8 ft. Long; ¼x10 in. Foot Steel Boards; ⅜ in. Heavy Adjustable Chain Hitch.

All-Steel Construction; Angle Iron Frame and Ends; Rivets used on Blade and Whereever possible; No Burrs to work loose; No Castings used except Lever Ratchets. Will stand the most severe strains and last for years; All Bolts in Bearings for tilting surrounded by Bearing Sleeves, making Levers easy to operate and permitting Bearing Bolts to be screwed tight without interfering with Tilting Device.

Nos.	+F436L	+F436L4
Size Frame, In.	3x3½	2½x2½
Weight Each, Lbs....	375	340
Each	$66.00	61.00

+Factory Shipment Only, F. O. B. Minneapolis

DRAG SCRAPERS

The Bowl is pressed from a heavy Plate of High Carbon Steel with smooth, hard surface that will scour perfectly in any soil; the Corners, Sides and Backs are formed on a gradual curve, allowing earth to roll in rapidly and making Scraper easy to fill to capacity.

Flange projecting around upper edge of Bowl makes Scraper 25 per cent stronger than Scraper without Flange; Center is full gauge thick; Solid forged Steel Bail; Heavy forged Steel Swivel turns freely in reinforced Socket, permitting sidewise dumping, if desired. Heavy Steel Hooks and Handle Sockets, securely riveted; Special hardened Steel Runners are fastened firmly with deep Countersunk Head Rivets.

Extra Bottom Plate attached firmly to Bottom with Countersunk Head Rivets; Best Quality Hardwood Handles, tapered to fit rigidly in Sockets.

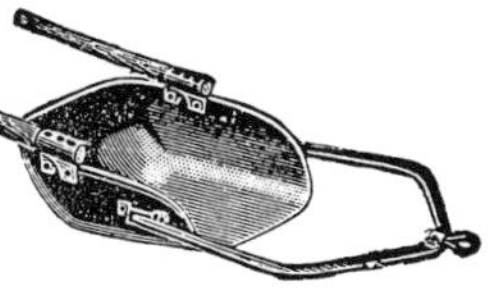

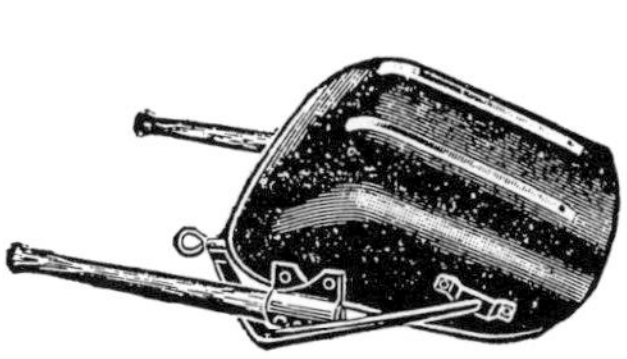

COLUMBUS PATTERN, SOLID STEEL

WITHOUT RUNNERS

Each

No. P436M—(1) For Long Hauls or down Grade; Capacity 7 Cu. Ft. of Earth; Size of Bowl, Top of Back to Cutting Edge, 34 in., Width 33 in., Depth 10 in.; Weight 95 Lbs. $15.30

No. P436M4—(2) For Ordinary Grading, Farm, Road or Township Work; Capacity 5 Cu. Ft. of Earth; Size of Bowl, Top of Back to Cutting Edge, 31½ in., Width 29½ in., Depth 9½ in.; Weight 85 Lbs. Each 14.70

WITH RUNNERS

Each

No. P436N—(1) For Long Hauls or Down Grade; Capacity 7 Cu. Ft. of Earth; Size of. Bowl, Top of Back to Cutting Edge, 34 in., Width 33 in., Depth 10 in.; Weight 100 Lbs. $16.30

No. P436N4—(2) For Ordinary Grading, Farm, Road or Township Work; Capacity 5 Cu. Ft. of Earth; Size of Bowl, Top of Back to Cutting Edge, 31½ in., Width 29½ in., Depth 9½ in.; Weight 90 Lbs. Each 15.80

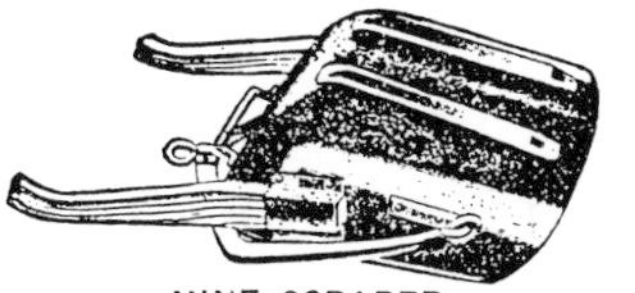

MINE SCRAPER

Special designed for use in mines or where space is restricted and winches and drag lines used for power. Heavy Steel grip is riveted to back of scraper for return pull either by hand or back haul drag line.

Body of scraper is pressed from a heavy plate of high carbon steel with hard, smooth, surface that scours freely.

Corners, side and back are formed on a gradual curve, making the scraper easy to fill. The swivel turns freely in reinforced socket, per- runners are heavy forged steel securely riveted. The swivel turns freely in reinforced socket, permitting sidewise dumping if desired.

The runners are specially hardened and are fastened firmly with deep countersunk head rivets. The handles are best grade hard wood with curved grip. Size of bowl, top of back to cutting edge, 30½ in.; Width, 26½ in.; Depth, 12½ in.; Gauge of steel, 12.

Each

No. P436Y —Without Bail, Wt. 47 Lbs....$12.90

No. P436Y2—With Bail; Wt. 53 Lbs....... 12.90

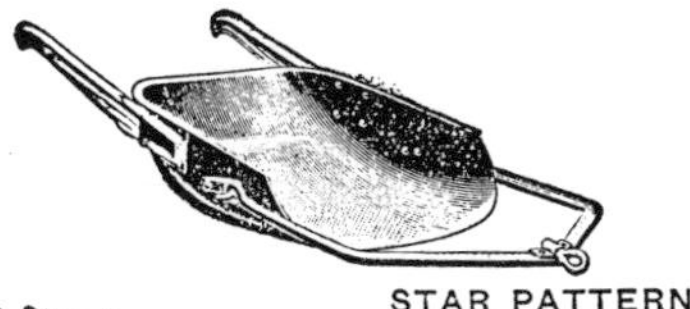

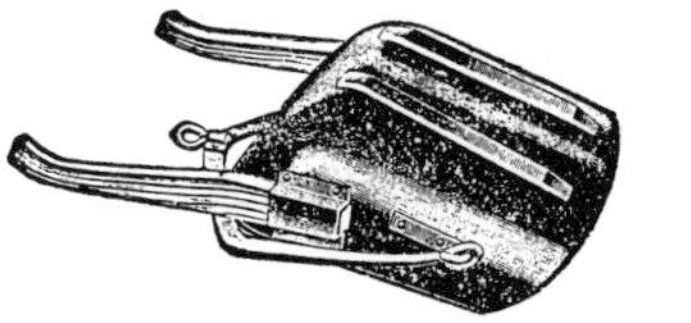

STAR PATTERN, SOLID STEEL

The Star Scraper is a medium priced Scraper of Lighter Weight than the Columbus; For Farmers and Township Use

WITHOUT RUNNERS

Nos.	P436P(1)	P436P4(2)
Capacity, Cu. Ft.....	7	5
Weight Each, Lbs...	80	76
Each	$12.40	11.80

WITH RUNNERS

Nos.	P436R(1)	P436R4(2)	P436R8(3)
Cap. Cu. Ft.	7	5	3
Wt. Ea. Lbs.	85	75	63
Each	$13.20	12.60	12.10

Note—No. P436R8 is for Narrow Ditch Work of Scraper.

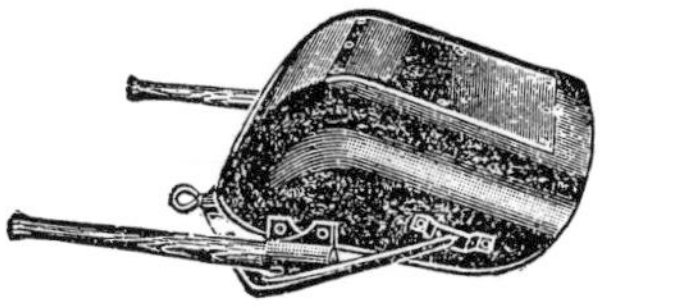

DOUBLE BOTTOM

With an **All Steel Extra Plate, 14x21 in.,** riveted to the bottom and curved up the back of Scraper.

No. ....P436T(1)

Weight Each, Lbs................ 105

Each $18.30

EXTRA HANDLES FOR DRAG SCRAPERS

Per Pair

No. P436V —Round; Full Size; Weight 4 Lbs. Pair..$1.00

No. P436V4—Square; Full Size; Weight 4 Lbs. Pair.. 1.00

Open Stock

209

Marshall-Wells catalog page showing drag scrapers, 1928.

Saw filer at work with his work bench, about 1920.

Skidding a log with tongs, about 1920.

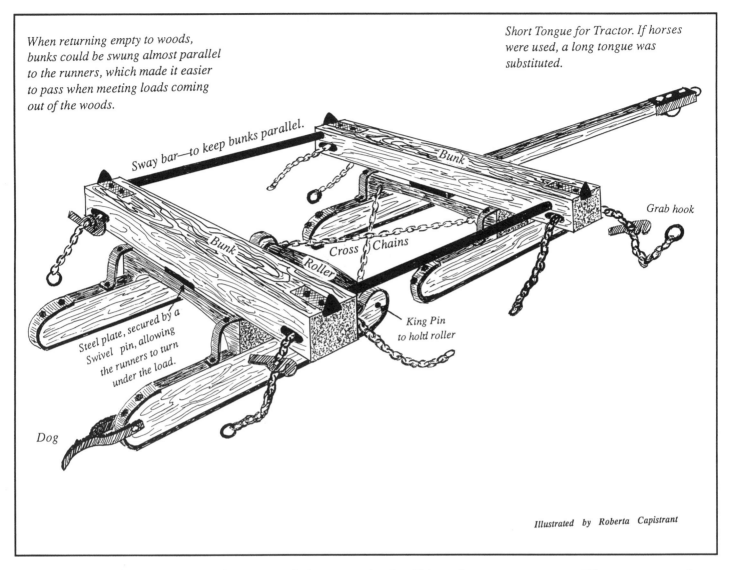

When returning empty to woods, bunks could be swung almost parallel to the runners, which made it easier to pass when meeting loads coming out of the woods.

Short Tongue for Tractor. If horses were used, a long tongue was substituted.

Sway bar—to keep bunks parallel.

Bunk

Grab hook

Bunk

Cross Chains

Roller

King Pin to hold roller

Steel plate, secured by a Swivel pin, allowing the runners to turn under the load.

Dog

Illustrated by Roberta Capistrant

Logging sleighs showing construction. Cross chains transmitted pull from front to rear runners. They were crossed so turning the front runners caused the rear runners to turn the opposite way and so follow the same track. The corner bind chains through holes in the bunks fastened the bottom outside log to the bunks with help from the spurs.

except that a single ring attached to the skidding chain connected the two handle rings. (see photo) Tongs were faster and easier to fasten and unfasten from the log than a choke loop in a chain or cable, but required a man to hold the tongs as they tightened.[76] Camp blacksmiths made tongs in the early days, but during the 1920s, KB bought most of its from Marshall-Wells' Duluth warehouse. Skidding chains usually had a grab hook at one end and a round hook (that would slide along the chain to make a choke loop) at the other end.

Logging sleighs offer a simple but highly developed example of practical engineering that withstood hard usage without undue failure. (See sketch)[77] An example from pine lumbering days, made in 1890 or earlier and recently recov-

ered from Avery Lake, is displayed at the Montmorency County Fairgrounds. Because it is essentially the same as sleighs used by KB during the 1920s, we can infer that the design had stabilized by 1890. Runners placed closer together than standard wagon wheels apparently allowed easier maneuvering around stumps and use of narrower roads. Apparently, the closer spaced runners did not reduce stability unduly. Some other companies used logging sleighs with runners much farther apart. This made them build wider, more expensive roads and made it more expensive to sprinkle their roads.

A set (or pair) of sleighs included a front and back sleigh. Each sleigh consisted of two steel-

**KLB Camp 1,
sleigh load of logs
about 1912.**

Logging at K.L.B. Camp 1.

shod, wooden runners three to four inches wide, eight inches high, and 82 to 86 inches long, held 49 to 56 inches apart by a round wooden rod called a "roller" at the front and an eight-by-twelve inch cross timber "bolster" just back of the center. The bolster had a vertical hole in its center for a single steel pivot pin that attached the "bunk", another eight-by-twelve inch wooden beam, which rode on top of and aligned (except when turning) with the bolster. Steel straps three inches wide and 0.75 inch thick fastened to the top of the bolster and top of the runners helped support the bunk when turning. Bunks were nine feet long for horse drawn sleighs, but twelve feet for tractor drawn sleighs; logs lay across the two bunks from front to rear. At the ends of the bunks, instead of stakes, 1.5-inch-long steel teeth called "spurs" helped keep the logs from sliding off. The main holding was by twelve-foot long chains called "corner binds" around only the bottom outside logs. Corner binds went through holes in and about ten inches from the ends of each bunk. Each corner bind had a ring at one end and a hook with a handle (called a "grab hook") fastened to the chain three feet from the ring, so the chain could be wrapped around the log, threaded through the ring, pulled tight and fastened quickly. In addition, a wrapper chain

attached to the middle of the sway bar was thrown over the whole load and fastened with a toggle for quick release. Sometimes, another chain already had been thrown over the load at half-height. A bent pole called a spring pole helped to pull the wrapper chain tight.

The front sleigh was attached to the back sleigh by wooden sway bars three inches in diameter, fastened between the bunks near their ends by clevises. In addition, one chain went from the right of the front bolster to the front of the left back runner and another chain ran from the left of the front bolster to the front of the right back runner. The crossed-over chains would thus both pull and steer the back sleigh.

Connecting the bunks and other parts together with chains and pivoting pins enabled the sleighs to travel over rough ground without large twisting stresses. The tongue was attached to the center of the roller at the front end of the front sleigh to steer it in the direction the horses or tractor took. A roller pivoted where it attached to the runners, so the tongue could move up and down freely. If a tractor pulled the sleighs, the tongue was only six feet long and reinforced with two steel bars running from the front of the tongue to near the ends of the roller of the front sleigh, where the bars connected through eyebolts to a pair of chains from

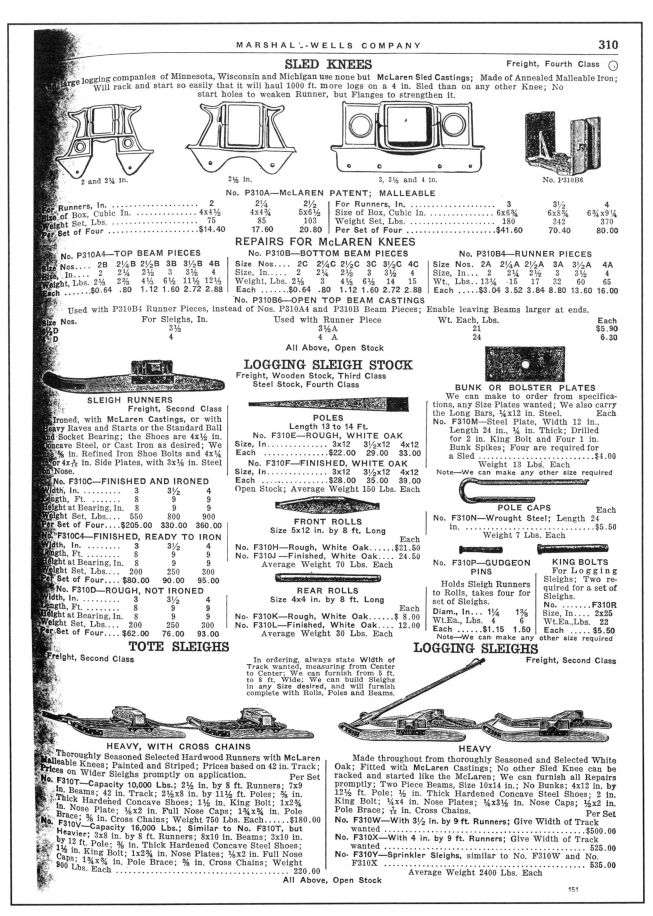

SLED KNEES

Freight, Fourth Class

Large logging companies of Minnesota, Wisconsin and Michigan use none but **McLaren Sled Castings**; Made of Annealed Malleable Iron; Will rack and start so easily that it will haul 1000 ft. more logs on a 4 in. Sled than on any other Knee; No start holes to weaken Runner, but Flanges to strengthen it.

2 and 2¼ in.　　2½ in.　　3, 3½ and 4 in.　　No. P310B6

No. P310A—McLAREN PATENT; MALLEABLE

For Runners, In.	2	2¼	2½	For Runners, In.	3	3½	4
Size of Box, Cubic In.	4x4½	4x4¾	5x6½	Size of Box, Cubic In.	6x6¾	6x8¾	6¾x9¼
Weight Set, Lbs.	75	85	103	Weight Set, Lbs.	180	342	370
Per Set of Four	$14.40	17.60	20.80	Per Set of Four	$41.60	70.40	80.00

REPAIRS FOR McLAREN KNEES

No. P310A4—TOP BEAM PIECES

Size Nos.	2B	2¼B	2½B	3B	3½B	4B
Size, In.	2	2¼	2½	3	3½	4
Weight, Lbs.	2⅓	2⅔	4⅓	6½	11½	12½
Each	$0.64	.80	1.12	1.60	2.72	2.88

No. P310B—BOTTOM BEAM PIECES

Size Nos.	2C	2¼C	2½C	3C	3½C	4C
Size, In.	2	2¼	2½	3	3½	4
Weight, Lbs.	2⅓	3	4⅓	6½	14	15
Each	$0.64	.80	1.12	1.60	2.72	2.88

No. P310B4—RUNNER PIECES

Size Nos.	2A	2¼A	2½A	3A	3½A	4A
Size, In.	2	2¼	2½	3	3½	4
Wt., Lbs.	13¼	15	17	32	60	65
Each	$3.04	3.52	3.84	8.80	13.60	16.00

No. P310B6—OPEN TOP BEAM CASTINGS

Used with P310B4 Runner Pieces, instead of Nos. P310A4 and P310B Beam Pieces; Enable leaving Beams larger at ends.

Size Nos.	For Sleighs, In.	Used with Runner Piece	Wt. Each, Lbs.	Each
3½D	3½	3½A	21	$5.90
4D	4	4 A	24	6.30

All Above, Open Stock

SLEIGH RUNNERS

Freight, Second Class

Ironed, with McLaren Castings, or with Heavy Raves and Starts or the Standard Ball and Socket Bearing; the Shoes are 4x½ in. Concave Steel, or Cast Iron as desired; We use ⅝ in. Refined Iron Shoe Bolts and 4x¼ in. or 4x⅜ in. Side Plates, with 3x⅛ in. Steel on Nose.

No. F310C—FINISHED AND IRONED

Width, In.	3	3½	4
Length, Ft.	8	9	9
Height at Bearing, In.	8	9	9
Weight Set, Lbs.	550	800	900
Per Set of Four	$205.00	330.00	360.00

No. F310C4—FINISHED, READY TO IRON

Width, In.	3	3½	4
Length, Ft.	8	9	9
Height at Bearing, In.	8	9	9
Weight Set, Lbs.	200	250	300
Per Set of Four	$80.00	90.00	95.00

No. F310D—ROUGH, NOT IRONED

Width, In.	3	3½	4
Length, Ft.	8	9	9
Height at Bearing, In.	8	9	9
Weight Set, Lbs.	200	250	300
Per Set of Four	$62.00	76.00	93.00

LOGGING SLEIGH STOCK

Freight, Wooden Stock, Third Class
Steel Stock, Fourth Class

POLES

Length 13 to 14 Ft.

No. F310E—ROUGH, WHITE OAK

Size, In.	3x12	3½x12	4x12
Each	$22.00	29.00	33.00

No. F310F—FINISHED, WHITE OAK

Size, In.	3x12	3½x12	4x12
Each	$28.00	35.00	39.00

Open Stock; Average Weight 150 Lbs. Each

FRONT ROLLS

Size 5x12 in. by 8 ft. Long

Each

No. F310H—Rough, White Oak......$21.50
No. F310J—Finished, White Oak.... 24.50
Average Weight 70 Lbs. Each

REAR ROLLS

Size 4x4 in. by 8 ft. Long

Each

No. F310K—Rough, White Oak......$ 8.00
No. F310L—Finished, White Oak.... 12.00
Average Weight 30 Lbs. Each

BUNK OR BOLSTER PLATES

We can make to order from specifications, any Size Plates wanted; We also carry the Long Bars, ¼x12 in. Steel. Each
No. F310M—Steel Plate, Width 12 in., Length 24 in., ¼ in. Thick; Drilled for 2 in. King Bolt and Four 1 in. Bunk Spikes; Four are required for a Sled $4.00
Weight 13 Lbs. Each
Note—We can make any other size required

POLE CAPS

Each

No. F310N—Wrought Steel; Length 24 in. $5.50
Weight 7 Lbs. Each

No. F310P—GUDGEON PINS

Holds Sleigh Runners to Rolls, takes four for set of Sleighs.

Diam., In.	1¼	1⅜
Wt.Ea., Lbs.	4	6
Each	$1.15	1.50

Note—We can make any other size required

KING BOLTS

For Logging Sleighs; Two required for a set of Sleighs.

No. F310R
Size, In. 2x25
Wt.Ea.,Lbs. 22
Each $5.50

TOTE SLEIGHS

Freight, Second Class

In ordering, always state Width of Track wanted, measuring from Center to Center; We can furnish from 5 ft. to 8 ft. Wide; We can build Sleighs in any Size desired, and will furnish complete with Rolls, Poles and Beams.

HEAVY, WITH CROSS CHAINS

Thoroughly Seasoned Selected Hardwood Runners with McLaren Malleable Knees; Painted and Striped; Prices based on 42 in. Track; Prices on Wider Sleighs promptly on application.
Per Set
No. F310T—Capacity 10,000 Lbs.; 2½ in. by 8 ft. Runners; 7x9 in. Beams; 42 in. Track; 2½x8 in. by 11½ ft. Poles; ⅜ in. Thick Hardened Concave Shoes; 1½ in. King Bolt; 1x2¾ in. Nose Plate; ⅛x2 in. Full Nose Caps; 1¾x¾ in. Pole Brace; ⅜ in. Cross Chains; Weight 750 Lbs. Each......$180.00
No. F310V—Capacity 16,000 Lbs.; Similar to No. F310T, but Heavier; 3x8 in. by 8 ft. Runners; 8x10 in. Beams; 3x10 in. by 12 ft. Pole; ⅜ in. Thick Hardened Concave Steel Shoes; 1½ in. King Bolt; 1x2¾ in. Nose Plates; ⅛x2 in. Full Nose Caps; 1¾x¾ in. Pole Brace; ⅜ in. Cross Chains; Weight 900 Lbs. Each 220.00

All Above, Open Stock

LOGGING SLEIGHS

Freight, Second Class

HEAVY

Made throughout from thoroughly Seasoned and Selected White Oak; Fitted with McLaren Castings; No other Sled Knee can be racked and started like the McLaren; We can furnish all Repairs promptly; Two Piece Beams, Size 10x14 in.; No Bunks; 4x12 in. by 12½ ft. Pole; ½ in. Thick Hardened Concave Steel Shoes; 2 in. King Bolt; ¼x4 in. Nose Plates; ¼x3½ in. Nose Caps; ½x2 in. Pole Brace; ₇⁄₈ in. Cross Chains.
Per Set
No. F310W—With 3½ in. by 9 ft. Runners; Give Width of Track wanted $500.00
No. F310X—With 4 in. by 9 ft. Runners; Give Width of Track wanted 525.00
No. F310Y—Sprinkler Sleighs, similar to No. F310W and No. F310X 535.00
Average Weight 2400 Lbs. Each

151

Marshall-Wells catalog page showing sleighs and their parts.

the front roller to the cross timber of the front sleigh. A steel "dog" at the back of the right rear runner could be pivoted down to a dragging position to stop the sleigh from sliding backward, or could be pivoted up to rest on the runner and not drag. Sleighs were not painted, but to retard rotting during the summer, they were kept off the ground, either run across poles or partly taken apart and stacked.

The blacksmith and the camp carpenter, called the "wood butcher," usually made sleighs in the camps, whenever they had time from their repair work. Sleighs differed in small ways depending on which blacksmith built them. Shoes for the runners came from Marshall-Wells' Duluth warehouse (see catalog page 310) already shaped and with a convex bottom. The bottom was convex so frozen-in sleighs could be worked loose by having the horses try to turn right and left. Shoes were a half-inch thick and came in 3, 3.5 and 4 inch widths with attaching bolts whose heads matched the convex bottom of the shoe. The wood butcher had to match the runners to the curve of the shoes while the blacksmith made the other steel parts of the sleighs. When the shoes wore out, the whole sleigh was considered worn out. Logging sleighs were also called bobsleighs or a "pair of bobs" instead of a pair of sleighs. This was because they used two sets of shortened, i.e. "bobbed" runners instead of

one set of runners the whole length of the sleigh as in earlier times. A pair of bobs was much easier to turn than sleighs that had full length runners.

Marshall-Wells supplied all sorts of things (except clothing and groceries) needed by loggers, mines, and industry, and vital to operations in remote places. When KB asked Marshall-Wells about telephones and wire for use at Camp 20, the supplier replied with a detailed list of what would be needed.

Special snowplows, sometimes called road rutter-plows, manufactured in Cheboygan, Michigan, and Eau Claire, Wisconsin, (see catalog page 309) made ruts eight to twelve inches wide in the ice roads to keep the sleigh runners on the road.[78] A wheel on top controlled the depth of the ruts, making them deeper for a slope than for level ground. The plow's wings threw the ice and snow to the side of the road; it would also be used whenever debris or snow accumulated on the road, before or after sprinkling. Plowing the snow aside kept the sprinkler water on the road and let the ground freeze underneath so it could support heavy loads. Logging sleighs had only seven or eight inches of ground clearance between their runners, so they could not operate in deep snow. Snow rollers used for town and farm roads played no role in logging.

The Overpack Company in Manistee manufactured the first big wheels used for logging,

Road rutter snowplow ahead of a load of lumber for Camp Six. Horses named Boney and Barney each weighed a ton and were the biggest team KB had. 1908. Photo by J.E. McC.

Kneeland & Biglow Lumber, Co.   114" OF T.
Lewiston Mich. 1908.

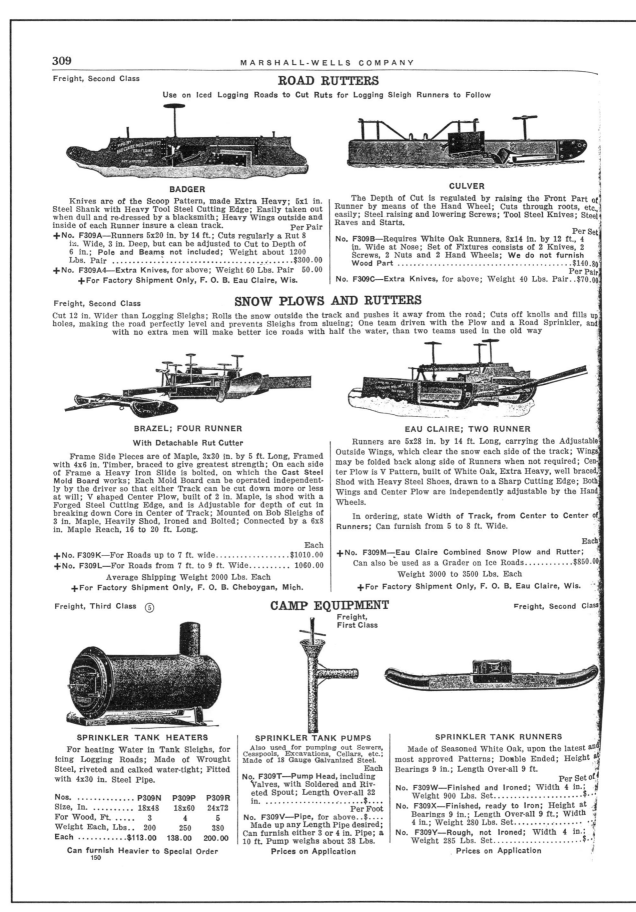

Freight, Second Class

ROAD RUTTERS

Use on Iced Logging Roads to Cut Ruts for Logging Sleigh Runners to Follow

BADGER

Knives are of the Scoop Pattern, made Extra Heavy; 5x1 in. Steel Shank with Heavy Tool Steel Cutting Edge; Easily taken out when dull and re-dressed by a blacksmith; Heavy Wings outside and inside of each Runner insure a clean track.   Per Pair

+No. F309A—Runners 5x20 in. by 14 ft.; Cuts regularly a Rut 8 in. Wide, 3 in. Deep, but can be adjusted to Cut to Depth of 6 in.; Pole and Beams not included; Weight about 1200 Lbs. Pair $300.00

+No. F309A4—Extra Knives, for above; Weight 60 Lbs. Pair 50.00

+For Factory Shipment Only, F. O. B. Eau Claire, Wis.

CULVER

The Depth of Cut is regulated by raising the Front Part of Runner by means of the Hand Wheel; Cuts through roots, etc., easily; Steel raising and lowering Screws; Tool Steel Knives; Steel Raves and Starts.
                                                            Per Set

No. F309B—Requires White Oak Runners, 8x14 in. by 12 ft., 4 in. Wide at Nose; Set of Fixtures consists of 2 Knives, 2 Screws, 2 Nuts and 2 Hand Wheels; We do not furnish Wood Part $140.80
                                                            Per Pair

No. F309C—Extra Knives, for above; Weight 40 Lbs. Pair..$70.00

Freight, Second Class

SNOW PLOWS AND RUTTERS

Cut 12 in. Wider than Logging Sleighs; Rolls the snow outside the track and pushes it away from the road; Cuts off knolls and fills up holes, making the road perfectly level and prevents Sleighs from slueing; One team driven with the Plow and a Road Sprinkler, and with no extra men will make better ice roads with half the water, than two teams used in the old way

BRAZEL; FOUR RUNNER

With Detachable Rut Cutter

Frame Side Pieces are of Maple, 3x30 in. by 5 ft. Long, Framed with 4x6 in. Timber, braced to give greatest strength; On each side of Frame a Heavy Iron Slide is bolted, on which the Cast Steel Mold Board works; Each Mold Board can be operated independently by the driver so that either Track can be cut down more or less at will; V shaped Center Plow, built of 2 in. Maple, is shod with a Forged Steel Cutting Edge, and is Adjustable for depth of cut in breaking down Core in Center of Track; Mounted on Bob Sleighs of 3 in. Maple, Heavily Shod, Ironed and Bolted; Connected by a 6x8 in. Maple Reach, 16 to 20 ft. Long.

                                                            Each
+No. F309K—For Roads up to 7 ft. wide.................$1010.00
+No. F309L—For Roads from 7 ft. to 9 ft. Wide......... 1060.00
          Average Shipping Weight 2000 Lbs. Each
     +For Factory Shipment Only, F. O. B. Cheboygan, Mich.

EAU CLAIRE; TWO RUNNER

Runners are 5x28 in. by 14 ft. Long, carrying the Adjustable Outside Wings, which clear the snow each side of the track; Wings may be folded back along side of Runners when not required; Center Plow is V Pattern, built of White Oak, Extra Heavy, well braced, Shod with Heavy Steel Shoes, drawn to a Sharp Cutting Edge; Both Wings and Center Plow are independently adjustable by the Hand Wheels.

In ordering, state Width of Track, from Center to Center of Runners; Can furnish from 5 to 8 ft. Wide.

                                                            Each
+No. F309M—Eau Claire Combined Snow Plow and Rutter; Can also be used as a Grader on Ice Roads...........$850.00
          Weight 3000 to 3500 Lbs. Each
     +For Factory Shipment Only, F. O. B. Eau Claire, Wis.

Freight, Third Class ⑤

CAMP EQUIPMENT

Freight, First Class   Freight, Second Class

SPRINKLER TANK HEATERS

For heating Water in Tank Sleighs, for icing Logging Roads; Made of Wrought Steel, riveted and calked water-tight; Fitted with 4x30 in. Steel Pipe.

Nos.	P309N	P309P	P309R
Size, In.	18x48	18x60	24x72
For Wood, Ft.	3	4	5
Weight Each, Lbs.	200	250	330
Each	$113.00	138.00	200.00

Can furnish Heavier to Special Order
150

SPRINKLER TANK PUMPS

Also used for pumping out Sewers, Cesspools, Excavations, Cellars, etc.; Made of 18 Gauge Galvanized Steel.
                                                            Each
No. F309T—Pump Head, including Valves, with Soldered and Riveted Spout; Length Over-all 32 in. ....$....
                                                          Per Foot
No. F309V—Pipe, for above..$....
Made up any Length Pipe desired; Can furnish either 3 or 4 in. Pipe; a 10 ft. Pump weighs about 38 Lbs.
          Prices on Application

SPRINKLER TANK RUNNERS

Made of Seasoned White Oak, upon the latest and most approved Patterns; Double Ended; Height at Bearings 9 in.; Length Over-all 9 ft.
                                                        Per Set of 4
No. F309W—Finished and Ironed; Width 4 in.; Weight 900 Lbs. Set....................$...
No. F309X—Finished, ready to Iron; Height at Bearings 9 in.; Length Over-all 9 ft.; Width 4 in.; Weight 280 Lbs. Set.................
No. F309Y—Rough, not Ironed; Width 4 in.; Weight 285 Lbs. Set.....................$...
          Prices on Application

Marshall-Wells catalog page showing snowplows, rutters, and sprinkler equipment, 1928.

called logging wheels or a set of wheels. Later, Gaylord Manufacturing in Gaylord made logging wheels,[79] although a few may have been made in the camps. The wheels usually ten— but sometimes eight—feet in diameter turned on an eight-foot axle with a fifteen-to sixteen-foot tongue. They could travel over rough ground with space to carry a "bunch" of logs under the axle. Logs were prepared for hauling by bunching across a pole so a sling chain could be pulled under them with a hook on the end of a rod called a "canary" and then around them when loading the wheels. Earlier model logging wheels had an eyebolt with either a hook or a chain-fastening link, attached to the front of the axle when used by KB, but to the top for some other companies. A "sling" or "bull" chain fastened to the eyebolt and draped over the top and back of the axle. When the tongue was raised a little past vertical, there was enough chain to go around the logs and back over the axle to hook on to the front of the axle. The teamster lifted the tongue while the loading crew pulled down on the tailboard, a two by ten inch board trimmed to be somewhat pointed at its tail end and extending one or two feet behind the tongue. Just one end of the tailboard

was fastened to the top of the tongue, three to five feet in front of the axle, with a clevis and chain link to an eyebolt, so the tailboard could be moved out of the way of the bunch when the tongue was up and propped by the tailboard.

After loading, the horses pulled down the tongue, thus raising the logs and making the load ready to move. Wrapping a chain around the back end of the log and tailboard helped stabilize the load. The teamster walked ahead of the loaded wheels and behind the horses, but when without a load, he often rode on the tailboard. If the wheels started to go too fast, the teamster would grab the near horse's breeching strap to help himself run faster and keep up with the horses. When hauling a load, the evener was fastened to the end of the tongue. (An evener is a strong board 40 to 48 inches long that connects the two horses' whippletrees so they can pull the same load at the same time with an equal pull from each horse. A whippletree connects a horse's trace chains to the load to be pulled or to the evener. Some people call the combination of evener and two whippletrees a doubletree.) If the wheels went faster than the horses, the trace chains from horses to tongue became slack and allowed the tongue to

Logging wheels with tongue up for loading, southwest of Gaylord, 1925.

Photo by Wm. Kuenzel

Logging wheels with load, front view showing chain around tongue, southwest of Gaylord, 1925.

go up and the logs to drop to the ground, slowing the load.

Freeman Parker described his experience hauling beech logs only eight feet long with logging wheels: The sling chain would not hold on the smooth beech bark, so he could not have the logs dragging to hold the load back on downhills. Instead he had to carry the logs balanced, not dragging. The horses were very nervous about the wheels behind them, so when they felt the trace chains slacken, they speeded up. Parker tried to catch hold of the breeching to help himself along but missed. One log came loose, then the wheels tipped over so he was lying under them but unhurt.

For unloaded wheels, fastening the evener to the tongue just ahead of the wheel rims and attaching the neck yoke to the front end of the tongue provided better maneuverability for backing the wheels over the bunch of logs.

Later models avoided unhitching the horses and lifting the tongue by using a "fingerboard" on a pivot attached just forward of the axle.[80] While the fingerboard was in a vertical position, the logs were attached to its lower end. The evener of the whippletrees was then attached to the upper end of the fingerboard so that when

the horses started, they pulled the fingerboard to a horizontal position where it latched thus holding the logs off the ground.

Steel "rub rings" on the inner side of the wheels protected spokes against damage from swinging logs.[81] Spokes—merely planed two-by-six inch boards— still needed replacement occasionally, so the KB mill in Bay City made and shipped them to the camps in lots of 100. The wooden rims consisted of nine segments called felloes held together by six-inch-wide steel tires. Each felloe was fastened to two spokes and was sawed to shape, not bent. Replacement felloes were bought from the Overpack Company, or in an emergency whittled out by Andy Allen, the locomotive engineer. Logging wheels stayed outdoors the entire year so their wood deteriorated, although they were repainted occasionally.

Operating logging wheels was dangerous and the men who drove them were considered daredevils. One KB logging wheel driver, Bill Currie, served as a Browning Automatic Rifle man in World War I, a job for the same type man. (Later he settled down to being a top loader and raised a family.)

Use of logging wheels decreased during KB's last years because fewer teamsters would dare

Logging wheels hauling a load, southwest of Gaylord. Notice absence of a stabilizing chain around logs and tailboard in back view,. 1925.

One-bunk dray.

Loading logs onto a one-bunk dray, about 1920.

A very big load of logs on a one-bunk dray, about 1920.

Photo by Wm. Kuenzel

Tractor pulling "truck" or wagon at new Camp 2, S.W. of Gaylord. George H. Vincent riding, 1925.

Ford tractor equipped with crawler tracks and pulling sleigh, about 1925.

their dangers.[82] Logging wheels were replaced by one-bunk drays (see sketch) that carried several logs supported two feet from their front ends by the bunk and with their back ends dragging. On level ground, the logs were more nearly balanced. The six-foot-long bunk fastened by a single pivot pin to a cross timber across steel-shod runners was low enough so a man with a cant hook could roll logs onto it up a ramp beam equipped with grousers so the logs would not slide down. At the top of the bunk, strong steel spikes (called grousers) sticking up about two inches helped retain the logs, together with a chain wrapped around the logs and bunk then fastened to the whippletree for pulling so it would be tight. A team of horses was hitched to the dray without a tongue; instead, a forked chain had two ends fastened to the outside of the runners and the third end fastened to the evener of whippletrees. The camps or the Stock Farm blacksmith shop made drays and log trucks. Drays could not be used if the ground was too soft or there was too much snow, whereas wheels could be used in mud.

KB employed a harness maker to make its horses' harnesses from the best quality leather

and fittings. He also kept the harnesses in nearly perfect repair. Teamsters sometimes polished
the leather and added their own brightly col-
ored celluloid rings to the harness and reins to
give them distinction.

About 1920, KB began using crawler tractors
to move logs.[83] In September 1924, KB paid
$6975 (FOB Peoria) for a ten ton "Logger"
crawler tractor to replace one purchased two
years previously, which had in turn replaced an
earlier tractor. Answering a Ford Motor
Company inquiry, Lunden wrote in 1924 that
KB had ". . . two Holt crawler tractors and three
Ford tractors equipped with crawler treads in
use, but the Fords were too light and only
worked well on fairly level ground. One Ford
was equipped with a winch to pull logs out of
holes and over hills. The Holt tractors would go
up any grade with a load of three to four thousand feet of maple on a pair of sleighs, and on
reasonably level road they would handle two or
three sets of sleighs."[84] During winter, dena-
tured alcohol protected tractor radiators from
freezing.

There were several ways to load logs onto a
vehicle:

• Cross-hauling, so called because a team
  of horses hauling crosswise of the vehicle
  rolled a log up skid poles with a chain.
  (see photo) The chain ran from the whippletrees over the log and back to fasten
  on the vehicle. In other kinds of material
  handling, the technique is called par-
  buckling. The advantage of this method
  was needing no equipment except flexi-
  ble chains imported from England,[85] or
  light-weight cables could also be used.
  The disadvantages were: There was danger to the men who put the chain around
  the logs if a chain broke or came loose.
  Also, the horses needed space to maneu-
  ver.

• The "A-jammer", a horse-powered
  arrangement of cables and pulleys on
  poles (see sketch) was a simple but effec-
  tive log loader. (Probably it was called a
  jammer because an arrangement of ropes
  and pulleys had been used to clear log
  jams on rivers.) An A-frame made of

Cross haul loading a railroad car; horses are out of sight at left, about 1920.

Photo by Wm. Kuenzel

Loading a log truck with an A-jammer southwest of Gaylord. Notice width of wheel rims and absence of floor in log truck. Horses are pulling cable to raise log. Two men are holding chains fastened to hooks. G.H. Vincent supervising, 1925.

A-Jammer loading logs onto a log truck.

Loading logs onto decks with a Russel swing-boom jammer, southwest of Gaylord, ca. 1923.

poles twelve-to fourteen-feet high supported a large pulley, which in turn supported the cable for lifting logs. The A-frame was mounted at one end of eight-foot-long skids on the ground. An adjusting pole going from the cross bar on the "A" to the other end of the skids adjusted the angle of the A-frame to project it over the destination of the logs when working or to balance it over the skids when moving. The cable through the pulleys had one end attached to the whippletree evener of a team of horses, the other end had a "Y" with two hooks far enough apart to fasten to the ends of a log. Two "hookers"—men who set the hooks—carried them to the log to be moved and set them, then the log was dragged and lifted to its destination. Skid poles ran from the ground to the top log on the load to guide the log to the top of the load. Ropes attached to the hooks enabled the hookers to guide the log down properly onto the load or pile, on signal from the "toploader" who stood on top of load and was responsible for packing the logs tightly, to fill all the space.

• Russell swing-boom loaders were based on a vertical pole with a pivoting hori-

Becker Patent Steam Log Loader at Old Camp 1, and Herman Lunden, about 1903.

Loading with slide back steam loader, New Camp 2. Two men on ground are holding lines to hooks, 1925.

zontal boom at its top so it operated as a crane, powered by either horses or an engine-driven winch. Russell loaders were made in the camps, perhaps with metal parts from the Russell Foundry. They required more work to move and set up than A-jammers, so were usually used to lift logs from sleighs and trucks to decks. (see photo) The decks of logs could be twenty feet high, so the toploader needed great skill to place logs at the edge of the deck so they would not roll down and scatter the deck. Usually, a deck would only collapse when logs thawed that had been piled while frozen.

• Steam-powered log loaders were of different types, depending on how they moved from one railroad car to another. The Raymond Slide Back Loader sat on skids on one flatcar while loading the car in front of it, then winched itself to the next car by pulling on a cable or chain fastened to that car. Its boom could not swing, so it could only be used to load railroad cars. (see photo)

• McGifford Self-Propelling Log Loaders,

intended for loading logs on railroad cars, had four outboard wheels on a frame that made it possible to lift itself over flat cars and move to another car. McGifford type loaders had other uses: KB equipped one with a scoop to load sand into a railroad car for railroad rebuilding.[86] Log loaders helped take up railroads by picking up the rails and loading them onto cars.

When loading railroad cars, KB began using steam powered cranes called "jammers" or log loaders in October 1901. (see photos) Steam powered log loaders required an operator with a steam engineer license. A log loader and crew could load ten cars per day in 1927.[87] The MCRR owned a loader and rented it to logging companies.

Log-measuring scale rules were small but important pieces of equipment used to make a quick measurement of the number of board feet that could be sawn from a log. They looked like a yardstick with a handle. The scaler laid the log rule along a diameter at the small end of the log, with its far end at the inside edge of the bark. Then, using the rule, at the other inner edge of the bark of the log he could read the approximate number of board feet from the scale for the length of the log. KB used the Scribner version log rules considered more

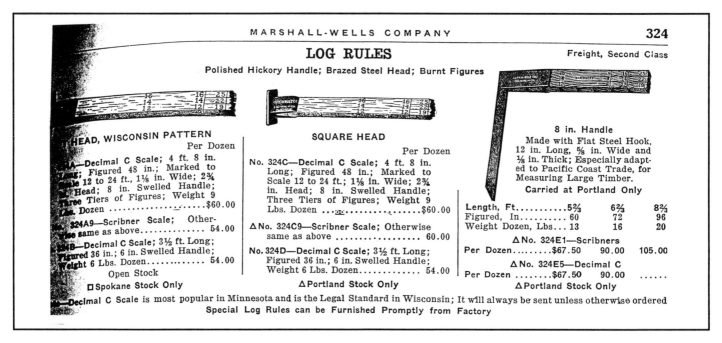

Part of Marshall-Wells page showing Log Rules, 1928.

accurate than the Doyle version. A sawmill's efficiency could be estimated by how much its output exceeded or fell short of the scale of logs going into it.

KB operated in a period of rapidly changing techniques and equipment. Following an earlier advertisement for a Carbide gas-powered starter for automobile engines, Herman Lunden's 1925 papers contain advertisements for four-wheel-drive cars, snowmobiles, snow removal machinery, and chainsaws. KB apparently used none of these except a snowmobile. There are photographs that appear to be of tests of a tractor for pulling log trucks, however.

Logging With the Railroad

KB logging operations completely depended on railroad transportation of logs to its sawmills and therefore centered where a railroad could be built. KB's first camp was 4.2 miles north of Lewiston's Salling Avenue and a quarter mile west of County Road 491, on the Davidson Branch of the MCRR where a short spur went to the east. (See map) The Davidson Branch started at Vienna Junction, 0.4 mile west of Buttles Road, just south of Salling Avenue, and continued in a generally northerly direction into Vienna Township (T30N-R1E). KB soon advanced the railroad to Gaylanta Lake (formerly Lake 22) and its second camp was built between the main track and a spur line on the southwest side of the lake. Next, the company extended the railroad farther north, entering the upper KB Valley and reaching Camp 3, built at the place labeled Donnelly (after the camp foreman) on the United States Geological Survey map.[88] (This was the site of an Antrim Iron Company wood cutting camp in 1938.) The railroad then turned south, following the east side of the Valley about 2.5 miles to Camp 4, then went on another mile to Camp 5, and finally two miles to Camp 6 where it ended. Later, KB built a spur from Camp 3 north and west to Camp 8. A quarter mile north of Camp 4, a spur line started south along the west side of the Valley for a mile. Half a mile north of Camp 4, another spur went easterly three miles to the Camp 9 swamp along Barger Creek, then northwesterly past the site of the KB Stock Farm into sections 13 and 12 of T30N-R1W.[89] North of

Camp 9, another spur went along Barger Creek, continued north past Big Rock, then spread out into several spurs. Many years later, the Big Fill spur of the railroad ran west from a point midway between old Camps 2 and 3 to Camp 22 and Camp 23, the last KB built. Seventeen of KB's camps were located along the Davidson branch or its spurs.

Much of KB's success in logging derived from Lunden's knowledge of terrain, allowing him to lay out feasible railroad routes to collection points (banking grounds) for log decks. Logs needed to be moved only short distances, mostly downhill, from cutting sites to the banking grounds. During the early period of operation along the Davidson branch, the railroad sent out a train of empty flat cars every morning from Lewiston to the camps and banking grounds. Every evening the train came back with thirty flat cars loaded with logs. (KB shipped fewer carloads in the 1920s because the cars were larger; then nine cars of logs would run the Water Street Mill for one day and one night shift.)[90] Often the crew would stop the train just outside Lewiston and wait to enter town until it was late enough for the crew to be paid for a full day. On the following day, the loaded cars joined the mixed train going to Grayling and went on to the sawmill at Bay City.

Information is available to describe the railroad layout in detail for Vienna and Briley Townships, but not for operations in Otsego and Cheboygan counties, which must have been similar. In the latter area, KB used the Detroit and Charlevoix Railroad from Frederic to Alba, the Michigan Central Pencil Lake branch, the McGraw branch between the Johannesburg branch and the BCG&ARR, the Newell branch near Wolverine, the Haak branch, and others. (Railroad branches are listed in the appendix.)

The railroad from the woods to the mills in Bay City was in effect part of KB's production line. Although KB was an important shipper, paying $283,446 for log freight and $320,832 for lumber freight in 1924 alone, a thread of conflict with the MCRR runs through KB correspondence. KB complained of not getting enough cars when needed, while its customers complained of irregular deliveries; for example, six cars one day but none the next instead of the two cars per day KB shipped. The MCRR complained of much more traffic in winter when its operating costs were high, than in summer when costs were lower, and of cars not fully loaded, which increased the number of cars it had to haul. Vagueness in railroad rates sometimes sparked strenuous negotiations about the applicable rate in a particular case. Log freight charges were based on the railroad's scale of board-feet on the car in the Lower Peninsula but on weight in the Upper Peninsula. Disputes also occurred over the amount of rail recovered from abandoning spurs.

When Frank Buell ran KBB, he allowed railroad crewmen to take things from his company store in order to keep their cooperation. Herman Lunden stopped this practice when he took control of the KBB logging operation, and instead sought cooperation from higher management of the MCRR. He overplayed this once by "chewing out" the MCRR division head in Bay City, who retaliated by refusing to send any cars to KLB sidings, making it necessary to order cars without using Lunden's or KLB's name. The feud between the two lasted until another man became the MCRR Mackinaw division head.

The MCRR maintained track and operated trains over the Davidson branch until 1925, when it decided to stop, although KB still had enough timber along the branch to employ two camps for four years. During the conflict over the Davidson branch, MCRR embargoed freight for a short time to all KB sidings, including those not on the Davidson branch. Apparently,

MCRR did so to make the Davidson branch appear unused so it could be abandoned, although Camp 8 was still operating and Camp 22 was about to start. KB got an injunction to restore service,[91] employed E. L. Ewing, a consultant on dealing with the railroad, and asked the Bay City congressman for help. After long and bitter negotiations, KB agreed to take over construction, maintenance, and operation north of the doubling (passing) track at Sarvey, four miles north of Lewiston.[92] KB also agreed to get its logs and wood out so the last track could be taken up by June 1, 1929.

Ending branch service allowed an MCRR crew to come from its base at Grayling to Sarvey, leave empty cars, pick up full cars, and be back in Grayling during an eight-hour day, instead of basing a locomotive and crew in Lewiston. Ending MCRR service on the branch allowed KB to build railroad to a cheaper standard than MCRR required and thus KB could afford to build more railroad and less sleigh road.

The MCRR leased a locomotive to KB for $5 per year, with KB responsible for all maintenance. KB wanted its train crew to pick up the locomotive at Grayling,[93] but MCRR refused to let the KB crew operate on its track between Grayling and Sarvey. Instead, MCRR wanted payment for a full train crew consisting of engineer, fireman, conductor, and brakeman. Finally, KB got the locomotive shipped to Sarvey at the regular freight rate, towed with the side rods to the drive wheels removed.

A loaded car of logs weighed from 25 to 35

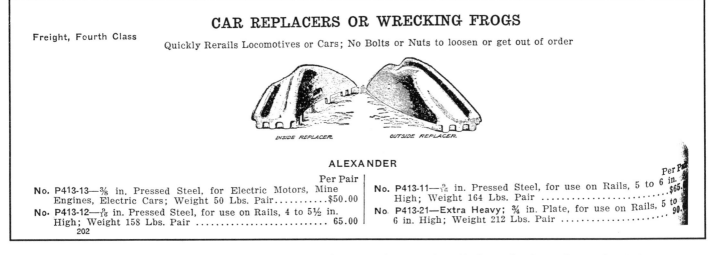

Part of Marshall-Wells catalog page showing wrecking frogs used to put de-railed cars back on the track, 1928.

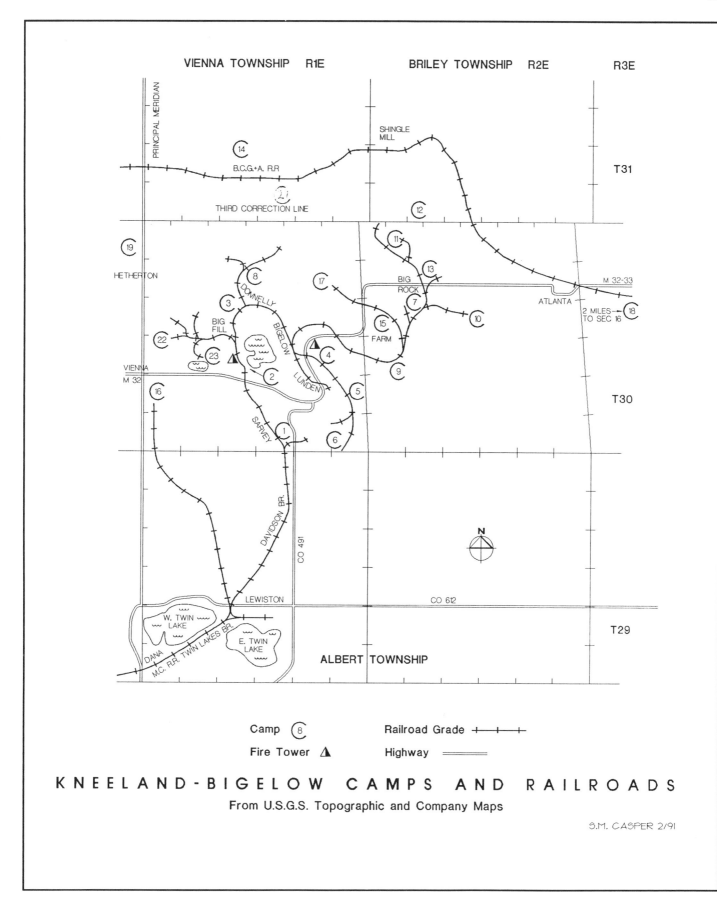

KNEELAND-BIGELOW CAMPS AND RAILROADS

From U.S.G.S. Topographic and Company Maps

S.M. CASPER 2/91

Kneeland-Bigelow Camps and Railroads.

tons, so the roadbed need only be strong enough to support that weight, if the locomotive were light also. MCRR furnished KB an overly large, over-the-road locomotive that used five or six tons of coal per day instead of the one-and-a-half to two tons required by a suitable locomotive. Extra costs to KB included excessive fireman's time and treated boiler water. If those high costs had continued for the remaining four years of KB's operation, the company would have been better off buying two suitable locomotives at $6000 each. Moreover, badly worn wheel flanges allowed the locomotive to go off the track too easily. A device called a "frog" (see catalog page 413) then had to be placed under the wheels to guide the locomotive back onto the track. Lunden wrote that KB needed a locomotive of about thirty tons, low geared,[94] short coupled, with small wheels, and not top heavy [that is, not a saddleback type]. MCRR had nothing to match these specifications, but they offered to let KB try a B-82 switch engine for two or three weeks. The switch engine proved satisfactory and KB rented a "flanger" type snowplow from the MCRR. The engine had a steam aspirator so it could pump its own boiler water from either Gingell Lake or Double Lake. Operating the locomotive on the Davidson Branch cost $100 per day in 1927.[95] Logs went from Sarvey to the mill in Bay City in two days.

KB's troubles with the MCRR were not yet over, however. Railroad management had invested in cars able to carry heavier loads and wanted to use as few cars as possible to reduce operating costs. On the other hand, train crews wanted to use as many cars as possible for longer trains and more jobs. Train crews considered cars with long stakes to hold tall loads dangerous, and American Railway Association Instructions prohibited their use. However, they could be used on MCRR track.[96] The logging companies found themselves in the middle of this dispute. Train crews blamed the companies for wanting long stakes, when they really opposed them because of the significantly increased cost of the stakes, difficulty of high loading, and loss of logs that fell off, particularly along the rough logging spurs. The train crews refused to accept cars if the stakes leaned

outward noticeably. This seemingly impossible problem was solved by tying the stakes together across the load with number nine steel wire when the car was three-quarters full, then piling on more logs, that had to be big and heavy to hold the wire tight.

The railroad then insisted that stakes on the cars be a minimum of five feet, four inches long, and fit the pockets on the cars closely. Until this time, stakes were made in the camps by splitting short logs, but splitting such long stakes to fit the pockets was impractical and used the best straight-grained logs, so stakes had to be made in the sawmill and shipped to the camps.[97] Stakes were usually manufactured seven feet long, but were cut off at the car floor level when unloading, becoming a foot shorter with each use. The cost of stakes, plus the danger to the men unloading cars by cutting stakes at floor level, persuaded KB to move a log loader to the Bay City sawmill for unloading logs. Evidently this idea proved unsatisfactory, because in June 1928 the loader was shipped to Camp 20. During 1928-29, KB crews usually could not load the 4000 board-feet required by MCRR on each car without the load becoming unstable, so MCRR charged KB a penalty for under-loading.

In April 1927, KB recovered an accumulation of 25 carloads of its logs unloaded from cars requiring repairs in Grayling. KB finally got the logs shipped on to Bay City only with the help of a new Railroad Division Manager.[98] The Johannesburg Manufacturing Company also had difficulty with the MCRR. KB's relationship with the BCG&ARR and the Soo Line seemed much smoother.

To take up railroad track, a small crew and a steam log loader would go to the far end of the spur track and then work back to the main line.[99] Workers would pull the spikes on just one side of the rails and unbolt them. The log loader would pick up the rails and put them on a railroad car. If a new spur track was to be built, the spikes would be taken up and used again, otherwise they might be left on the grade because they had only scrap value.

Lumbering Personalities

Leonard Hayes operated a Lower Peninsula mill for sawing railroad ties.[100] Once Hayes

Old Camp 3, men, buildings, and railroad track, about 1908.

excused himself from a conversation when he saw two of his crew together loading one tie at a time into a boxcar. He began loading ties all by himself and his crew soon followed his example, one man to a tie.

In December 1924, the men setting hooks in logs for the loader lacked the skill to put a second tier of logs on the car and threw down their hooks and walked off the job. Herman Lunden (at age 65) and George Vincent (at least 55) set hooks for half a day, until more skilled hook setters arrived. Lunden took pride in his ability to do anything in lumbering except cook. He kept its logging so up-to-date and well managed that forestry professors brought their classes to see KB camps and operations.

Lumber companies settled cases of their crews cutting other company's timber with stumpage payments, unemotionally and without recourse to the courts. Perhaps this was because the men who did the actual cutting did not benefit from it, and a company could find itself on the other side of the issue the next time.

There seemed to be no concern about the number of relatives KB employed. For example, Richard Thompson and his four sons worked for the Company; as did George Vincent, his two sons and cousin, Charles; James White and his son Fred. Four of Herman Lunden's nephews worked for short times as scalers.

Logging Camp Life

Camp locations are listed and a typical inventory summarized in the appendices. Camps were built next to a railroad and banking ground because much of the work would be done there. KB camps usually each had 50 to 75 men, with 60 considered the most efficient size.[101] In 1910, KB and KBB together operated ten camps during the winter employing 600 men in the woods.[102] At least three or four camps operated year around. The last KB camp built was number 23, but KBB & KLB had another series of camps and after the 1922 merger, a new series with just three camps began. Camp 20 was actually two camps four miles apart, plus a camp for peeling hemlock bark. In sum, KB and KLB together had a total of about forty camps.

Later KB camp buildings usually were of roll-roofing-covered boards, not logs, because logs had become too valuable to use in construction without sawing into lumber. Camps used lots of water for men, horses, and sprinkling iced roads, so location on a creek was desirable before gasoline engines were available for pumping. Camps lacked bathrooms.[103] Electric lights in the logging headquarters—and in camps built after about 1920—came from 32-volt storage batteries, each in sixteen big glass jars, charged from electrical generators powered by a Delco one-cylinder gasoline engine.

**Logging crew.
Foreman wears
necktie, cooks
wear aprons,
about 1908.**

Photos by John D. Cress

Camp 4, 20 horses and log barn, Chas. Turner at right, 1910.

A hard-working foreman ran the logging camp without any intermediate foremen between him and the men. "If a man needed much supervision, he was soon replaced. The foreman could usually see the whole show twice a day and have time left over to check the cooks, barn boss and blacksmith."[104] According to Lunden, "There is no one paid less [$135 to $150 per month plus room and board] for his hard work than a Woods Foreman . . . As a rule he is on his feet from four in the morning to seven or eight at night, Sundays and all."[105] Camp foremen were rated on the basis of what it cost them to get a thousand board-feet of logs cut and loaded on railroad cars. Some foremen considered especially good at getting buildings built and roads laid out usually started camps, while other foremen would run camps at later stages of production life.

The scaler provided administrative assistance, in addition to his principal task of measuring with a log rule and recording the number of board feet in each log of a pile or carload. With a marking hammer, he placed the owner's mark on the small end of each log. Additionally, the scaler prepared paperwork for railroad shipments, ordered supplies, forwarded invoices for supplies received to the purchasing department in Bay City, and did timekeeper and accountant reports for the logging headquarters. He also ran the "van" (a contraction of "wanigan", the shanty on a raft that carried supplies on river drives) that was a small branch of the company store, selling tobacco, candy, socks, etc. The "wood butcher" repaired and made wooden parts for equipment such as sleighs, canthooks, and whippletrees, all much more durable than could be bought from suppliers. Tool handles and whippletrees probably were made from ironwood, which must be shaped soon after cutting because it becomes too hard to work after drying. A barn boss[106] oversaw care of the horses, feeding them at 4:00 a.m. so they would finish eating at the same time as the teamsters, cleaning the stables, and checking horses' shoes and feet regularly to make sure no trouble was developing. He took care of sick horses and dosed them if they had colic. A blacksmith repaired equipment, built new equipment when not repairing, and kept ten to fourteen horses properly shod. A good horse shoer was easily forgiven any shortcomings in other skills. Horses were valuable, as a good team could cost $900, ten months wages for the blacksmith. Blacksmiths were likely to stay only a few months in the camps but remained much longer at the Stock Farm, so they did more difficult work there. The smith at the Springvale camp was noted for making log-marking hammers that were unusually deeply incised by chisel, grinding wheel, and drill so the scaler did not have to hit the log squarely to make a complete mark. KB marking hammers had shorter handles than those pine loggers used, as well as smaller letters (7/8 inch high instead of 1-1/2 inch), because they did not have to identify logs in the water.[107]

Food in the camps was very important to successful operation, because if lumberjacks disliked the food, they would leave for a camp that had better meals. Men who did this physically very demanding work had to be well fed.[108] KB fed its workers at a cost of about twenty cents per meal, including salaries of all cook camp people. Cooks received a bonus for keeping costs down. The highest paid cook in 1926, a woman at new Camp 2, received salary and bonus of $160 per month, plus room and board—more than the camp foreman was paid. During December 1927, new Camp 2 served 6297 meals at an average cost of $.164 each. KB found that feeding quality food was more economical and less wasteful than using cheap food. Cheap canned goods had excessive

Photo by John D. Cress

Camp 10, 14 horses, 2 oxen, George E. Vincent in front. Building construction has changed since Camp 4. 1910.

water; cheap meat was mostly bone. Dried fruits, particularly prunes, were served often. Hundreds of bushels of apples were used every year, and their cores from lunches started apple trees to mark former banking grounds. Cooks had to bake bread in each camp because they were far from bakeries. Horses were more expensive to feed than men, as the following table shows:

The cost of feeding men and horses in December 1928 was:			
Camp 2, SW of Gaylord:			
3103 meals	$0.218 per meal	451 horse-days	$0.770 per day
Camp 20, North of Rexton:			
7074 meals	$0.204 per meal	620 horse-days	$0.691 per day
Camp 22, East of Gaylord:			
6375 meals	$0.203 per meal	904 horse-days	$0.761 per day

In July 1912, meals had been even cheaper, because food prices were lower and there was less variety. The cost of meals for KLB men then was:

Camp 1   2439 meals at $0.149 per meal
Camp 2   4058 meals at $0.1475 per meal

Traditionally, the lumberjacks did not talk during meals in order to avoid starting fights. Common food items included "square timbers," large, sugared cookies baked in a large pan and cut into squares. Lunden sometimes brought guests to the camps for meals. Men who were traveling through, called stragglers, could get a free meal for helping the chore boy at a logging camp.

(Left and Right photos) New Camp 2, southwest of Gaylord, 1925.

Mr. and Mrs. Miller, the woman cook blowing horn to call men, 1925.

Cook camp with men coming, southwest of Gaylord, 1925.

Cook camp inside another camp, about 1920.

KLB Camp 1, Charley Craner and wife in dining room, newspapers for insulation, lamp for light, ca. 1915.

The men drank coffee only at breakfast, using much more tea than any other beverage, probably because people had become accustomed to drinking tea when it was cheaper than coffee.[109] Tea leaves came in sixty-pound wooden chests lined with sheet lead. Tea was prepared in the camps by dumping tea leaves into a five-gallon kettle filled with cold water, bringing the kettle to a boil, then pushing it to the back of the stove to steep. Men going into the woods put a handful of tea leaves into a gallon jug of drinking water when starting the day. The water would be much more palatable for quenching thirst than plain water left to stand and become warm.

Cook camps had some conveniences. Pipes carried water from a storage barrel to a heating coil in the cookstove. The hot water then ran to a large sink that went across one end of the building and drained into a seepage pit. The choreboy washed the dishes for sixty men in about forty-five minutes, using speedy techniques. In some camps, the dishes, after being scraped off with a spatula, went into a fifteen- or twenty-gallon galvanized-steel washtub with hot water and Gold Dust soap powder. The plates were not stacked but tossed into the tub, so some were upside down and some on edge, then stirred with a stick to wash them.

After stirring, the wash water was poured off, and almost boiling rinse water was poured on. After the rinse water was poured off, the dishes and cups were put on racks to air dry. Knives, forks, and spoons, washed and rinsed in the same way, but separately from the dishes and cups, went into an empty cloth grain bag, which was swished around on a table to dry them. One chore boy helped the cook, carried water, and kept the fires going. Another chore boy cleaned the men's camp (bunkhouses), cut firewood, and kept the fires going.

Albert Stoll[110] reported a meal at KB Camp 2 southwest of Gaylord as follows:

A feast was set before us. Roast beef, roast pork, stewed corn, creamed peas, baked beans, homemade bread and butter, potatoes, two kinds of preserves, stewed prunes, canned peaches, homemade doughnuts and cookies, and tea. There was oodles of it, piled high on the rough tables. And such food! Cooked like our grandmothers cooked. 'Is this the regular layout?' inquired the photographer, [Wm. Kuenzel]. [H. Lunden answered] "Absolutely, we feed this way three times a day and seven days a week. How do you like that beef? Every pound of meat used in our camps is raised on our stock

Mess tent, George H. Vincent in white apron, 1914.

farm. That beef is the finest produced, coming from registered Aberdeen-Angus cattle. The same holds true of our pork and mutton. We make our own butter, and the cook does every bit of baking. In this camp we have 65 men. The cook and his good wife handle this food job all alone. Do you think that lumberjacks are well fed?" We had to admit that they were not only well fed, but over-fed.

When the company hired extra teams of horses from local farmers, part of the payment customarily included dinner at the camp for the farmer and his horses.

David Clink[iii] writing in the Montmorency County Tribune during March 1969, described life in a KB lumber camp as follows:

Life in the lumber camp was not like living at home, but the K-B Company made it as comfortable as possible for their men. The camp was composed of several buildings, each one serving a necessary function for the efficient operation of the camp, and each one designed to make the lumberjack's task more palatable.

Probably, to the lumberjacks, the most important building was the "cookhouse" or mess hall. It was built in the shape of a "T". The dining room was the horizontal part of the "T" while the vertical section held the kitchen and a storeroom, which also served as a place for the cooks to sleep.

The cook's day began at 4 a.m., when he began preparing a breakfast of flapjacks, eggs, bacon, and lots of hot coffee. Immediately following breakfast, the cook's concern was preparing the noon meal. If the loggers were too far from the camp to travel back for lunch, the cooks prepared a hot meal and took it out to the cutting area …The meal was placed in a wooden insulated box and loaded onto a sleigh or wagon and taken into the woods. The food was served on tin or granite [enameled steel] dishes…

After a ten-hour day in the woods…the lumberjacks at the KB Camps were more than ready to settle around the fire in their bunkhouses. Each bunkhouse held about 30 men and contained one large stove placed in the center of the long building. It was around this stove that tales of the lumber camp originated. Next to the stove was a barrel where water was kept warm by the heat of the stove. Usually, near the end of the building was a wooden sink that served as a wash basin for the lumberjacks. Along each side of the bunkhouse were long rows of wooden bunks which were covered with straw. The straw served as a mattress, and if a pillow was desired, a grain sack was filled with hay…

One of the remarkable things about the KB Company's logging equipment was the fine character of the teams employed in the woods work, grading, etc. The horses were a vitally important factor in the work of logging in this area, and the KB Company took great pride in keeping its teams in excellent condition. A number of their two-ton teams were considered among the finest in the state. The KB teamsters were known for the care and special attention they gave their equine co-workers…

The most important asset of any logging operation was that group of independent, jovial, devilish men known as lumberjacks. They came and went as they pleased, and often shifted to another company for a change of scenery. The camps formed a little village in and of themselves and afforded accommodations such as were found in few places. Because of this, the class of workmen in KB camps was far above average . . . Aside from the local men who worked in the camps and went home Saturday night, the lumberjacks seldom left the camp from one week to the next.

Lumberjacks had a great reputation for carousing after being paid, but work as a lumberjack was a good way for more sober men to save money to pay for a farm or business. The men who went straight home with their pay attracted no attention. Some men did not draw all their pay as earned but let it accumulate. Most people who worked for KB received a monthly wage instead of piecework pay. Lumberjacks looking for work in the woods often started at the sawmills, which were easy to find, relatively close together, and from which they could get directions to camps that were hiring. Usually, the lumberjack's attitude was to get lots of work of done, striving to outdo other men and crews in production as befits men whose hero was Paul Bunyan. But men would leave camp to attend important local events like the Otsego County Fair.

Lumbering crews worked ten hour days, six days a week without much regard for bad weather, but did not work in November rains. During winter weather, the lumberjacks' footgear consisted of rubber overshoes over heavy wool socks, over light felt boots, over wool socks. In summer, some men wore winter underwear believing it would keep them cool. Working without regard for the weather was carried so far that twice during one winter, Baldy Sanford poured babbitt metal to replace the main bearings in a tractor where it broke down in the woods. Herman Lunden wrote[112] of mud a foot deep, and horses and wheels so muddy one could not tell what color they were. Two teams of horses had to be used on each set of logging wheels and the men were soaking wet from the waist down, although supplied with rubber boots.

Career progression in the logging industry usually occurred as follows:

A lumberjack started as a swamper, clearing trails and roads. Next, he might become a sawyer, which required learning to fell trees so they would not hang up on another tree, but fall in a direction where they could be picked up and hauled away. The next step was to be a teamster driving horses. Progress then became slower, either learning the camp's paperwork and becoming the scaler or advancing to foreman. (A scaler might also progress to foreman.) A foreman who worked for a company with more than one camp might progress to walking boss or woods superintendent. An alternative path was to become a jobber/logger employing lumberjacks and owning equipment, contracting to cut timber owned by others. Often, the jobber could get along without much capital by getting an "advance" from the timber owner to pay for equipment and building a camp. The timber owner had to have faith in both the abili-

ty and integrity of the jobber. A jobber might become able to buy standing timber, cut it and sell the logs to a sawmill. The final step was to own both sawmill and timber. This last step required substantial capital, probably obtained by combining or merging with a sawmill owner.

Monthly pay rates reflected that progression. In July 1925, for instance, they were (in addition to food and housing):[113]

- $30 to $40 for swampers, choreboys, helpers
- $50 to $60 for sawyers, teamsters
- $70 to $75 for scalers
- 80 to $90 for top loaders
- $90 to $110 for blacksmiths
- $80 to $160 for cooks
- $155 for the accountant
- $160 for the logging superintendent

Forest Fire Control

Forest fires were a perennial problem for lumbermen. A fire could wipe out their timber investment at any time, and an early spring fire could destroy their working capital in camps and logs awaiting shipment. Before organization of the Michigan Conservation Department, the Michigan Hardwood Manufacturers' Association maintained a cooperative to fight forest fires on members' land, hired a fire warden, and stationed him at either Deward or Gaylord. The Northern Forest Protective Association operated similarly in the Upper Peninsula, assessing its members a half cent per acre for fire protection.[114]

Several of Lunden's letters to Bigelow mention fighting forest fires. For example, he wrote: "Fires are raging everywhere, but we are holding them. None of us on the Davidson Branch has been in bed since Monday, but it is under control, and nothing is lost."[115] Before there was a Conservation Department, KB built its own fire towers and manned them during hazardous times. The first (before 1923) steel firetower in Michgan—consisting of three legs with an open platform—was located on a hill about 800 feet northeast of Bigelow.[116] Another was about a quarter mile north of Lunden Lake in Section 22. Before using steel towers, KB used tree platforms for observers as described below:

> To Herman Lunden of Gaylord, pioneer lumberman and one of Michigan's fore-

most "conservationists" belongs the credit for erecting the first fire tower in the State as a means of establishing better fire protection for his timber holding.

In 1896, Mr. Lunden had built a lookout tower in the tall elm tree at the top of a hill overlooking a large tract of timber in Montmorency County, 22 miles east of Gaylord. The "tower" consisted of a large platform supported in the crotch of the elm tree and reached by a ladder made of two tamarack poles cleated together.

While the tower had no modern means of communication, . . . Mr. Lunden's watchman had a field glass to spot the fires, while at the foot of the tree he had two horses saddled and ready for use.[117] (This probably did not occur as early as 1896, more likely 1906.)

In a speech[118] on fire prevention about 1925, Lunden said:

I have been interested in fire prevention since childhood because the same thing which exists here today existed in one of the European countries [Sweden] when I was a child. My father was the author of the first forest fire bill that was passed in his native country. I have fully investigated their success, and know that they have had wonderful results, and the townships and counties have been well paid. . . . The one great enemy we have to combat is fire, and I will reiterate what I have often said before: that if we had kept the fire out of our growing timber and places where timber should grow, there would never have been need for a great program of reforestation in this country.

Once, when a camp was surrounded and threatened by forest fire, Lunden had the men put wet blankets on the roofs so the buildings would not catch fire from falling sparks. While he served as a Conservation Commissioner in 1923-6, his biggest interest was in forest fire prevention and control. He traveled with the Conservation Department's Forest Fire Flyer train educating people to prevent forest fires. In December 1925, he served on a committee that recommended that the State maintain at least three airplanes for locating fires.

Logging Headquarters at Bigelow

A junction point on the railroad—called Bigelow on maps and KB locally—developed seven miles north and one mile east of Lewiston at about the center of early KB operations. In what follows, I use Bigelow for the location to avoid confusion with the company. From about 1906 until 1929, it was the location for the KB logging operations office, where the "pencil gang" (accountant, clerks, storekeepers, traveling scalers, and logging superintendent) worked and lived. Here too, was the company store/commissary, which purchased supplies for the camps, stored supplies (a $12,000 inventory and $70,000 annual sales, mostly personal items for the men), and distributed them as needed. It also special ordered things for employees. The nearest store was four miles away at Big Rock. These functions occupied an unpainted, rambling structure 90-by-52 feet overall (see sketch).[119] It contained a store, a cold room with ice stored above it, a tin lined flour storage room, a general office, a large safe, Herman Lunden's office, a scalers' office, a bunk room, electric generator room, and considerable warehouse space. The pencil gang ate at a two story boarding house. There were houses for the logging superintendent, the accountant, the scalers, and other workers. A root cellar stored food that would be damaged by freezing, a small barn sheltered the driving horses used by the staff, and other buildings housed a harness maker's shop, a platform scale, and a coal bin. (They burned coal at $6 per ton plus transportation, instead of using wood for fuel.) When KB bought hay or potatoes from local farmers, they delivered at Bigelow where the drive-on scale weighed wagon or truck loads. From a concrete water tank buried in the hill east of the store, a pipe ran to a standpipe in front of the boarding house where a hose could be connected to fight fires. A springhouse built over Staninger Creek, a quarter mile south of the Store, kept perishables cool in summer. The Vienna Township Hall also was at this center of population. In 1994, only one of the houses remained, in proximity to a more recent vacant gas station with grocery store and repair shop.

The need for the Bigelow site is difficult to understand now, but when KB began, roads

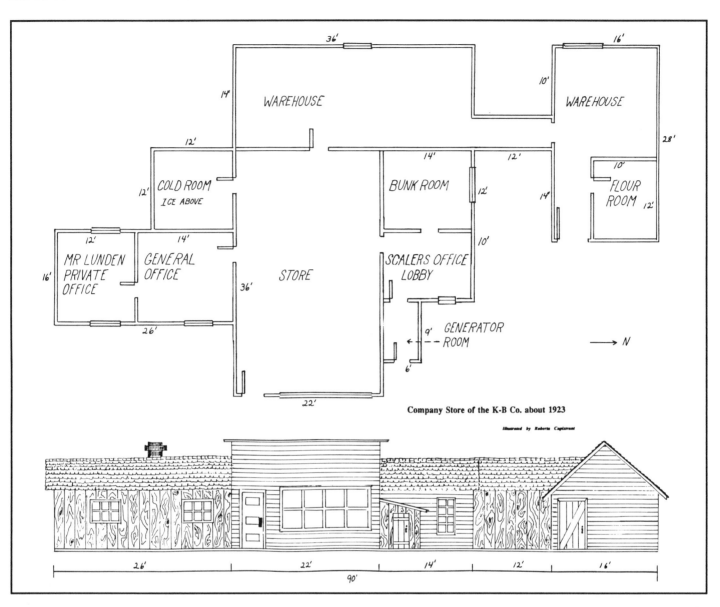

Company Store of the K-B Co. about 1923

Illustrated by Roberta Capistrant

Company store of the K-B Company about 1923.

were very poor and trucks non-existent, so the company needed a convenient headquarters and supply base on a railroad. About 1918, Bigelow became inconveniently located for Lunden, so he rented an apartment and office for himself over the bank in Gaylord. Gaylord was more nearly the center of his operations by then, and had much better telephone service than did Bigelow, as well as two north-south passenger trains and one east-west train each day. By 1927, Bigelow had three cars and a truck for modern transportation. A new Cadillac purchased every year for Mr. Bigelow was eventually assigned there.

In May 1925, Mr. Bigelow wrote that KB employed about 200 men in Bigelow and the nearby camps. The staff at Bigelow was headed by George E. Vincent, Sr., who had started as foreman at old Camp 1 and became logging superintendent (walking boss), continuing with KB until he died in 1937. William A. Humphrey was the highly regarded accountant, until he became ill in 1928 and Fred J. White took over his duties, in addition to serving as store manager. Everyone was in awe of Mr. Humphrey with his formidable personality, stand-up desk, and skill in accounting. He also had a Victrola and stacks of classical records in his house. The store manager was Thomas Milner until he became ill early in 1925 and was succeeded by Fred White. The boarding house was earlier managed by Lelah Winter, and later by Bertha Thompson, whose husband Ernie was the locomotive fireman. Charles D. Vincent was the surveyor, timber cruiser and chief scaler, assisted by Lawrence Manier and Uri Roberts. After

Vincent's death, Roberts became chief scaler and spot checked the measurements of all scalers. Traveling scalers would go to a jobber's location, measure what his crew had produced, and write a check for him on the spot. The barn boss was Isaac Smith, the harness maker was Charles Nichols, the delivery truck driver was Fred Vincent, the office clerk was Fannie Manier, and Sanford Hull was man-of-all-work and wood butcher. Cost accounting for the logging operation was taken very seriously to estimate each camp's production costs per thousand board-feet of logs shipped. A partner in a "Big Eight" accounting firm in 1984 looked at the company's operating statements and commented that: ". . . their detailed cost accounting seems quite sophisticated for a field operation."[120]

During the 1920s, many people lived around Bigelow, but could travel only with difficulty (especially women) during the winter, so they had weekly parties at the boarding house and dances at the Township Hall.[121] The stage driver who carried the mail between Lewiston and Atlanta would do shopping in town for people on his route and salesmen rode on the stage, which was a light wagon in summer and sleigh in winter. In the spring and fall, the stage used a sleigh from Lewiston to Bigelow and a wagon from Bigelow to Atlanta, where there was less snow.[122] People could ride the railroad caboose to Lewiston and then go to Grayling, or else catch a train in Johannesburg for Gaylord.[123] Bigelow's winter isolation ended in the fall of 1926, when Montmorency County began using two 1-1/2 ton International trucks equipped with Wausau V-plows to keep the roads clear of snow from Atlanta to Hillman and Lewiston.[124] In 1928, the county bought a crawler tractor that could get up the hill west of Bigelow when plowing the road to Vienna.

Kneeland-Bigelow Stock Farm

To solve the persistent problem of finding a reliable source of meat in the quantities needed for the logging camps,[125] KB followed the example of the Avery's lumber company, which operated one farm just east of Atlanta, and another near Hillman, as had the Pack's lumber company. KB developed Aberdeen Farm, named for the Aberdeen-Angus cattle breed kept there.

Rather than operate a stock farm, many companies fed the men lots of beans and salt pork, which could be transported and stored without much danger of spoiling, thus gaining a reputation for feeding lots of beans. Earlier era lumberjacks sang about "Louie Sands and Jim McGee who feed us beans three times a day." The farm had 340 to 350 acres under cultivation of a total of 500 acres considered cleared. Its buildings were located 1.75 miles east of Bigelow, mainly in the north half of Section 19, T30N-R2E, but most of its cleared and cultivated land was on both sides of M-32 east of Bigelow and along the access road. Section 23 contained fenced cattle pasture and there was "open range" in parts of Section 25 and 36 of T30N-R1E that supported 75 to 100 steers in summer, supervised by the herdsman. On November 3, 1926, 151 head of cattle were tallied in the barn with about ten strays outside.[126] KB also bought young cattle from local farmers in the spring to use its pasture. The company had a over 190 cattle in the spring of 1928. In addition to the registered Aberdeen-Angus cattle, the farm had a herd of sheep and about sixty hogs to supply the camps with young pigs for garbage clean-up and meat later. Originally, the farm grew some potatoes, wheat and oats, but after 1921 it concentrated on livestock.

Richard Thompson managed the farm until he became foreman at Camp 8, then William MacKenzie, and later LeRoy C. Fowler followed him.[127] Mrs. Fowler received her own paycheck at $0.25 per meal for boarding the farm crew. In 1928, time reports showed that the number of men working the farm varied from five, including the foreman, butcher, and teamster during winter, to eighteen men and thirteen horses in July. That crew also operated two small farms about three miles away.

The farm achieved a measure of fame for its exceptionally large barn, built in 1920 to replace a smaller one that had burned. The big barn was 66-feet wide by 160-feet long, plus a one story 40-by-44-feet concrete wing on its east. (see photographs)[128] It measured 80-feet high, from basement floor to roof, including a basement ceiling height of nine feet. An 18-feet high and 24-feet wide cupola as big as a small barn extended the full length of the barn to let light

The big barn from the west, ca. 1923.

into and hot air out of the haymow. Galvanized steel ventilators added atop the cupola in 1921 were connected by ducts to ventilate the basement. John E. Harrington of Gaylord was the builder.[129] Construction employed twenty men for six or seven months. Some people thought Herman Lunden extravagant to hire journeymen carpenters to build a barn, but he wanted to have the best as well as the biggest barn in Michigan. He sought advice from Michigan Agricultural College professors, so the barn was very well equipped. Tracks just below the cupola on both sides supported two "harpoon" forks that lifted hay from wagons and carried it to haymows. Litter carriers brought manure to a pit on the south side. Drinking water was piped to all stalls, which were floored with cork bricks for the cows' comfort.[130] Three rows of stanchions held cows, and a row of steel pens running the length of the barn held cattle up to two years old. Two 40-feet-high-by-16-feet in diameter silos stood on the barn's east side.

In the yard, a large Fairbanks-Morse gasoline engine located in a fireproof pumphouse 70 feet northwest of the barn pumped water and ran an electric generator. A gasoline engine inside the

The big barn, silos, and slaughter-house from east, ca. 1923.

Barnyard from northeast. Buildings left to right are: Big barn, foundation of burned barn, tool shed, ice house, granary, dynamo and pump house, big house, bunk house, 1920 or 21. This was taken from nearly the same place as the next photo, forming a panorama with a gap in the middle.

earlier barn was thought to have started the fire that destroyed it. (A temporary roof over the burned barn's foundation sheltered the cattle while the new barn was being built.) An 18-by-30-foot slaughterhouse was located immediately east of the barn and there was a 12-by-14-foot smoke house. (see photos) The big, former McClenathen farmhouse was about 100 feet northwest of the barn, with the men's bunkhouse 30 feet north of the house. A granary and icehouse were about 100 feet west of the barn. A 16-by-60-foot implement shed was about 50 feet southwest of the barn. Another silo and barn for young cattle was located about 300 feet northwest of the big barn and the 40-by-80-foot horse barn was 60 feet west of the barn for young cattle. Two big tanks, buried so they could never freeze, at the top of the hill south of the barn held a water reserve.

Because the farm showed a continuing loss of a few thousand dollars every year, Bigelow stopped its operation soon after logging operations finished in 1929. Farming generally had become unprofitable after 1920 and other people who tried large-scale ranching in northern Michigan found it unrewarding. After the sale of KB livestock during 1929, Leroy Fowler kept a small herd of his own cattle on the farm until about 1938. Then George Oswald became caretaker.[131] During 1943 and 1944, the barn's internal fixtures and the cork bricks were removed

and sold. The big barn deteriorated and was torn down about 1960.

A second, smaller farm with one house, two barns, and dairy cattle, was located three miles south of Afton on the east side of the Pigeon River. It was sold about 1930.

End of Logging

In March 1929, KB finished cutting its timber in the Lower Peninsula.[132] The last labor report came from Camp 23 on March 24, 1928, from Camp 22 and new Camp 2 on March 23, 1929. However, loading of posts and pulpwood continued through July 1929. After the last logs were shipped from the Davidson Branch, an MCRR locomotive and crew slowly pulled a log loader the five miles between Lewiston and Sarvey while a KB crew picked up 36 good logs that had fallen off along the track. A contractor finished pulling the KB steel on the Davidson Branch August 20, 1929 and returned the locomotive to the MCRR in Lewiston. The men scattered to find new jobs as lumbering in Michigan could no longer support them. Antrim Iron crews cut tree tops for chemical wood until 1930. The Water Street sawmill was dismantled. The flooring mill continued operation with lumber purchased from other companies' sawmills and the second-growth timber from T30N-R1E, until about 1937.

Railroad, office, sheep shed, horse barn, silo, black-smith shop, from southeast, about 1921.

During the summer and fall of 1929, KB equipment, supplies, horses and other livestock were sold, in some cases by auctions at the camps. The Antrim Iron Company bought much of the equipment, but the Gaylord Lumber and Fuel store got the walk-in safe from Bigelow. The task of supervising the shutdown and closing fell to Herman Lunden's son, Lester. After he finished, George E. Vincent, Sr. took over as caretaker for the northern properties and land sales agent. When Vincent became too ill to work, Uri Roberts took over in 1937. During the Great Depression, some former KB employees lived in KB housing at Bigelow and the stock farm.

A geologist, Lindberg, was hired to explore for minerals and petroleum possibilities in 1932-33. Frank Smith ran surveys and collected mineral samples about 1940. At various times, the KB Trust leased land to companies for oil exploration and drilling. None of these activities showed commercial possibilities, but after sale of the remaining oil, gas and mineral rights in 1965, significant quantities of oil and gas were found on former KB lands.

Charles Bigelow died June 10, 1932, then Pierson Kneeland bought his stock and took over management and control of the Company.[131] After he died in October 1942, Walter Wrape

became president, then the Bay Trust took over as trustee and began liquidating the company. Land not connected with Gaylanta Lake or the stock farm sold whenever there was a buyer. Most of the remaining land was sold in May 1946. The last of the Bay City real estate, the Belinda Street Mill site, was sold in September 1949 and is now a Chevrolet factory. The corporate name retained enough prestige to be attached to a lumber supply company. Sale of the residue of oil, gas, and mineral rights completed KB's liquidation.

Now, very little can be seen of KB. In Bay City, the building that housed the flooring or planing mill still stood in 1995, and at Bigelow a house, the big root cellar and barn foundations remain. In the woods are innumerable logging roads and many miles of railroad grade. Most KB lands are now in widely dispersed private ownership, but a large fraction became part of the Hardwood, Mackinac, and Pigeon River State Forests, with a small amount in the Huron National Forest. Much of the land KB lumbered still grows trees and supports elk, gas and oil wells. Some is being farmed, but most is used for recreation by hunters and fishers, modern-day beneficiaries of a once important, but now almost forgotten chapter of Michigan's hardwood lumbering history.

Blacksmith in his shop at KB Camp 4 about 1910. The big logs were typical of Camp 4 buildings The small two-shelf stand in the foreground appears to be a combination stand and tool carrier for horseshoeing. On the high shelf, there appear to be ball bats but more likely, they were cant hook handles. The photo seems to have been taken at night with flash.

Part III
APPENDIX

Appendix I
Kneeland-Bigelow Foremen and Jobbers

The camp foremen I can find mentioned were:

George E. Vincent, [Sr.] at old Camp 1,
Dan Ray at old Camp 2,
Joe Donnelly at old Camp 3,
Wally Really at Camps 5 & 6,
Richard Thompson at Camp 8,
John Brown at Camp 11
George Young at Camp 18
George H. Vincent, [Bub] at Camp 19, Springvale, and new Camp 1,
Robert Menzies at new Camp 3, and Camp 20,
Art Mosherman at new Camp 2, SW of Gaylord
John Allen at Camp 21?
James White at Camp 22,
Donald Deitz at Camp 23
Henry Germain
Clyde Gibbs at Camp 20
Wm. J. Merrick with KLB
Wm. Stauffer at KLB Camp 2

Jobbers who continued for several years during the 1920's included:

Leonard Hayes - Swamp timber and tie mill
Frank Thompson - Swamp timber
Peter Harper - Logs
Joe Shagonabe - Shingle Mill Operator
Alvie Jones - Shingle Mill Operator
Dirk Schreur - Logs
George Stevens - Logs
Sherman Manier
John Jackson

Appendix II
Kneeland-Bigelow Costs

The cost of producing flooring per thousand board-feet in 1928 was:

flooring lumber	$42.488
labor	$6.469
maintenance	$0.017
depreciation	$1.422
taxes	$0.495
general mill expense	$1.320
dry kiln	$5.072
power plant	$2.203
TOTAL	$59.486
average sale price	$63.628

The company made inventory adjustments at $60.257 per thousand, which came from averaging $59.486, with $62.607 per thousand, the cost of inventory on hand at the beginning of the year.

The cost figure $42.488 came from including the effect of shrinkage upon making flooring out of lumber costing $31.477 per thousand. The lumber shrank from 9,449,650 to 7,001,246 board-feet. This still seems inconsistent with a cost of $35.02 at the saw mill, unless substantially cheaper flooring lumber was purchased from another source.

During 1925, the planing mill processed 7,911,656 board-feet at a cost of $428,813, for an average cost of $3.641 per thousand.

Appendix III
Kneeland-Bigelow Camp Locations and Approximate Dates

1. T30N-1E, SE SE Section 34, where a spur went east from the Davidson Branch. 1901-03
2. T30N-1E, SE NW Section 22, between siding and Davidson Branch, SW of Gaylanta Lake. 1902-5
3. T30N-1E, SW SW NW Section 15, marked Donnelly on USGS maps. 1903-10
4. T30N-1E, NW SW SW Section 24, on McCormack Lake Road. 1905-13
5. T30N-1E, center of Section 25, SE corner McCormack Lake Rd. and Lutz Rd. 1906-08
6. T30N-1E, SW SW SE Section 36, near end of southern railroad grade. 1908-12
7. T30N-2E, SW SW Section 17, on railroad, (not fully equipped). 1911
8. T30N-1E, SE NE Section 9, NE corner of Old State Road and Camp Eight Road. 1923-26
9. T30N-2E, SW SE Section 19. 1910
10. T30N-2E, NW SW Section 16, Southeast of Big Rock. 1910-13
11. T30N-2E, SW Section 5, half mile north of Big Rock. 1912-13
12. T31N-2E, SE SE Section 32, on old Spiess place. 1912-13
13. T30N-2E, Section 8 east of railroad (probably a bark camp).
14. T31N-1E, SW SW Section 15.
15. T30N-2E, SE SW Section 18, Just across the road north of the big barn.
16. T30N-1E, NE Section 30, SW corner of Matthews Road and M-32.
17. T30N-1E, SW NW Section 12, On north side of Old State Rd.
18. T30N-3E, Section 16, 3/4 mile west and south of Teets' Corner.
19. T30N-1W, half mile north of Hetherton Church. 1924-25
20. T45N-8W, N NE Section 32, 1924 to 1927, became jobbers' camp.
20. T45N-8W, W NW Section 25, between Rexton and Soo Junction, 1927-9
21. T31N-1E, NW SE Section 27, just south of B.C.G.&A. 1923-25
22. T30N-1E, SW SW Section 17, one mile north of M-32 and a quarter mile east of Matthews Road. 1925-29
23. T30N-1E, NE SE Section 20, north shore of Double Lake. 1926-27

New KB Series
1. T30N-2W, NE SE Section 9, east of Gaylord on west side of M-32, on MCRR Ritska spur. 1922-26
2. T29N-4W, NE NW Section 10, on Hayes Tower Road. 1922-29
3. T31N-4W, Hallock, on BCG&A Railroad. 1924

KBB/KLB Series
1. T30N-1W, Section 5 or 6?? Johannesburg mailing address. 1911-12
2. T34N-1W, On Newell Branch of MCRR, southeast of Afton. 1911-12
12. T30N-1W, on Lake Harold Branch of Detroit & Charlevoix RR. 1912
? T33N-4W, halfway between Lake Louise and Springvale. 1922-25

Appendix IV
Inventories

There are inventories taken in 1928 for new Camp 2 and the Wolverine farm. The Camp 2 inventory is neatly written on 18 pages of legal size paper. It is broken down by locations, starting with the blacksmith shop, which had 214 descriptions from adz to wood chisels, listed at going-out-of-business prices. The barn included 10 teams of horses and a cow. There was equipment for growing potatoes, so evidently potatoes were grown at Camp 2. (Some of the land had been farmed earlier.)

LOCATION	NUMBER OF DESCRIPTIONS	VALUE
Blacksmith shop	214	$617
Pumphouse, Toolhouse, & Garage	53	$298
Men's Camp [bunkhouses]	23	$108
Outside Equipment	56	$2392
Barn	44	$1671
Tractor shed	51	$91
Harness room	51	$269
Office	100	$292
Cook camp	119	$166
TOTAL CAMP TWO	681	$5904
Farm N.E. of Wolverine	108	$1745

(This included 6 horses and 25 head of [dairy] cattle)

Aberdeen [Stock] Farm, on an insurance binder, dated July 23, 1926 had:

Dwelling #1	$2100
Dwelling	$1500
Blacksmith Shop	$1000
Barn #1	$17,500
Barn #2	$1500
Sheep barn	$2000
Granary	$1000
Two Silos	$2250
Machine Shed	$500
Bunkhouse	$500
Grain and seeds	$3000
Harness, Carriages, etc.	$2000
Hay, straw, etc.	$5000
Mowers, reapers, hayloader, etc.	$2600
16 horses at $200 each	$3200
75 cattle at ca. $75 per cow	$5000
Sheep	$1500
Hogs	$2500
TOTAL VALUE	$54,650

Appendix V
Logging Branch Railroads (Standard Gauge)

From the 1923 Land Book of the Kneeland-Bigelow Company and Trust

Main Branches		Spurs
Michigan Central Railroad Branches:		
Davidson	T29N-1E, T30N-1E, T30N-2E	Gingell: T31N-1E, Big Fill: T30N-1E; Lunden: T30N1E
		Donnelly: T30&31N-1E
Haakwood	T34N-2W	Hursts, Saddlers, Wylies
Johannesburg	T30N-1W	Ritska, McGraw, etc.
*	T31N-2W	
Newell	T34N-1W	
Page	T33N-1W	
Pigeon River	T33N-1W	
Richardson	T33N-1W	
Detroit and Charlevoix Railroad branches (owned by MCRR):		
Elmira	T29N-5W	
Hardwood	T29N-5W	
Lake Harold	T30N-5W	
Pencil Lake	T29N-4W	
Boyne City, Gaylord and Alpena Railroad:		
Green Spur		
Larson Spur		
Soo Line Railroad:		
Rexton		Hurds, Nine Mile, 443 and 449

* No name is available for this branch.

Description of a Saw Mill and Planing Mill at Rapid River, Michigan
For Sale by Wm. Haywood, Grand Rapids, August 3, 1927

[Describes a large lumber mill establishment whose equipment was powered by shafts and belts from a big central steam engine at a time when electric power was dominatng.]

Upstairs

Prescott Band Mill, 8 ft. wheels, takes a 45 ft. by 1 ft, 14 gauge saw
Arm guard for sawyer. Right hand

Deck can take logs up to 22 ft. in length. Automatic kickers. Steam powered log turner and also rig that kicks the log onto carriage.

Slide well built. Towards bottom rests on cement piers.
Lower part of the chain can be raised or lowered.

Prescott Edger. Four saws.

Live rollers lead from Band Saw the entire length of the mill and out through the end, so in case of striking a nail or anything, the log will go through the end of the mill where skids are built in and where a man with a cant hook can turn log off.

Chains connect from live rollers leading from band mill to edger, also from resaw to edger.

Resaw is Diamond Iron Works 6 ft. horizontal resaw. Takes saw 37 ft. 10 in. by 16 in., 16 gauge. Boards come from Tail Sawyer (just behind band mill). After boards are through, some go by chains to edger, balance requiring another cut come back by chains to resawer, returning on opposite side from those coming from band mill. Slabs developing are dropped immediately behind on slasher [saw], while good boards not requiring another cut go on to the edger.

Carriage is three block Prescott.

Slasher [saw] can take edgings or slabs twenty feet long without trouble. Four circular saws four feet apart built in the frame, that is, the saws are stationary, they are not raised or lowered. Slabs pass under shaft holding saws.

Trimmer can handle up to 22 feet, but at this length, one edge would be untrimmed. Will take 20 ft. and trim both ends. Saws are two feet apart and will trim four feet up to twenty feet. A feature of this trimmer is that at far end there are two saws, two feet apart, where usually there is only one saw at this end.

Hog: Do not know the size of this hog, but believe it is a Phoenix. Our practise has to depend on the hog almost entirely for fuel. Hog rests on cement base.

Lath mill: These are standard Lath Machine and Bolter. Used only for slabs suitable for lath. Capacity about 30 M lath per ten hours.

Downstairs

Very roomy. Cement floor. About 22 ft. from floor to ceiling. Large door at one end 8 by 10. Plenty of light so ordinarily, no lights are needed during the daytime. Three sets of stairs leading upstairs.

The main shaft as well as several other shafts rest on concrete bases, these bases being not less than six feet high. All timbers have been creosoted on the bottom and all are 12 in. by 12 in. in size and whitewashed. Many timbers also rest on concrete bases about 18 inches high.

Well equipped with conveyors. Upstairs, no rubbish or waste of any kind has to be transferred, there is always a chute or conveyor handy. Downstairs, one large conveyor leads to the fire hole, another to the waste burner. No rubbish accumulates, and no rubbish need be hauled out of the mill. Two men can oil, keep downstairs swept up clean, and do the bulk of the millwright work.

Plenty of overhead walks and ladders, so placed that one can reach any shaft or other piece of machinery without soiling clothes. Entire mill well piped for fire protection, both downstairs, upstairs, and in the filing room.

Belt room for belts and small parts, also an upstairs to the belt room; both rooms on lower floor.

At the west end of the downstairs, there is a clear space about 15 by 20 feet suitable for millwright work not requiring shop facilities.

Filing Room

Large, roomy, filing room [for filing saws], plenty of light, windows on north and south side of mill. Room is entire width of mill. Eight Hanchett Machines, including grinder for circular saws, shears, and retoothing machine, electric forge, also other machines. In addition to these eight machines, there are benches, tools and facilities. Hardwod floor. The band saw grinder can run by electricity as there is a motor for that purpose.

Blacksmith Shop

Double shop, that is, it is rigged for two blacksmiths working independently at the same time. Well stocked with tools. Machine shop in connection containing a planer, drill press, and hack saw. These machines run by steam. A steam engine fed with steam from the engine room does the work.

Pump House

This is a boiler which maintains pressure on the large pump independently of the boiler house of the saw mill. This maintains pressure on all the pipes in the mill as well as half of the yard.

Engine Room of Saw Mill

This engine is well kept up and has always furnished ample power to the mill. It is not a Corliss engine, but of a make that seems to be equally popular with steam men. Two 150 HP. boilers.

In this unit there is a 500 gallon Underwriters Pump made by Fairbanks-Morse. Also, a small pump in this unit that works independent of the large pump.

There is also another steam engine that runs the dynamo, which in turn runs a small dynamo [exciter?]. When any quantity of light is wanted, the steam engine is started and the mill generates it own lights. If only a light or two is needed, the city lights are turned on. The city light supply will take care of our entire requirements, if necessary.

In the boiler house there are two boilers of 150 HP. each. There is a separate stack for each boiler. The bulk of the fuel is hog feed. Last year we used only one or two loads of slabs a week in addition to the hog feed. The feed goes directly into the fire. When it comes too fast, it goes into bins. When the bins are full and no feed is needed, it is diverted to the waste burner conveyor.

Waste Burner

This burner is 21 feet in diameter and over ninety feet high. Screen on top. Refuse is dumped in a little more than half way up.

Planing Mill

Contains a lath mill unit at one end consisting of cut-off saw, splitter, bolter, lath machine, lath trimmer, besides other fixtures and equipment going with a lath mill.

Contains an S.A. Woods planer and matcher No. 20; Fisher resaw No. 4, taking a 29 ft. 3 in by 7 in., 18 gauge saw (although a six inch will work as well), a Berlin Planer and Matcher, a Byrkit Lath Machine and a rip saw.

Lath bolts for the lath mill can be unloaded from cars at the same time that planed lumber is going out of the mill into cars. Track right alongside mill.

Has a Brownell Co. engine, No. 6109, size 14 x 16 [bore and stroke in inches] This engine can run the entire lath mill and planing mill, but is little light to do this work steadily.

Has a large Corliss engine. Do not know the size, but it will easily run everything we have at both saw mill and planing mill. The Brownell engine is still hooked up, so in an emergency it can still be used. The large engine has a sixteen foot flywheel. The main shaft can be extended indefinitely in case more units are added. Also have a pump, so pressure is maintained in the planing mill as well as that part of the yard not served by the saw mill pump.

In addition, there is a large filing room with five machines. The equipment is ample for all the planing and lath mill requirements except the grinding of the band saws for the resaw. This is done at the big mill, and as that machine has an electric motor, the mill does not have to be in operation for this work.

There is an oil house for the planing mill, also one for the saw mill. Both these buildings are separate from the main buildings. We also have two warehouses near the planing mill, about 100 by 25 feet and 75 by 30 feet, a separate building for gasoline, a barn that can take care of 25 or 30 horses, two garages with a capacity of four cars, a boom house for boom tools, also an office building wth a firepoof vault.

The transfer at the mill is as level as a table, built on upright timbers standing on piles driven into the ground. The transfer is long enough to take care of hemlock, separating each size in Merchantable for length and width, four inch to twelve inch inclusive, eight to twenty feet, 8/4 #3 separated separately by widths, 4/4 #3 as it comes, 4/4 Mer. as it comes, with a truck or two for emergency if a few logs other than hemlock should be sawed.

We have two Russel flats, each with four wheel trucks, also two four wheel flats for general work. Have two tram tractors, Prescott tractors with Ford engines.

Have a tie hoist suitable for any kind of short stuff. The hoist is a Fairbanks-Morse gasoline engine of 15 horsepower.

Have about 4800 feet of trams with three loading docks. One of these docks will handle two cars, the others, one each. All three docks can be used at the same time without interfering with each other.

Plenty of trackage. Spur runs down to the two car loading dock, with switch and small spur alongside of which is a ground loading dock, which lets cars be loaded from the ground. All our loading docks have enough trackage so several cars can be loaded from each, every day. Have another track leading past the planing mill to the hoist, a distance of more than 2000 feet with two loading docks on it. Have a third spur leading past the mill more than 1500 feet long, of which the last 600 or 700 feet are a trestle for unloadng logs. This trestle is over the water and runs parallel to the bank, possibly 100 feet from the bank.

The lot our plant is on contains sixty to eighty acres. Additonally, there is an adjoining eighty acres available on long term lease.

References

1. Augustine H. Gansser, *History of Bay County Michigan*, (Chicago; Richmond & Arnold, 1905), pages 457-461, Biography of Charles A. Bigelow.

2. *Illustrated North American*, June 1912, pages 6,7,9 Biography of David M. Kneeland.

3. Herman Lunden, correspondence files, Bentley Historical Library, Ann Arbor, Michigan.

4. Lester C. Lunden, son of Herman Lunden and former KB executive, interview by author, Sep. 1, 1979.

5. Herman Lunden Miller, *Lewiston in the Lumbering Era*, 1992, page 15.

6. Wayne B. Welch, *Early Life in the Johannesburg Area*.

7. C.Bigelow to H.Lunden, June 26, 1928

8. H. Lunden to C. Bigelow, 5/24/28 indicates the Grand Rapids Trust broke up W.H. White & Co. well before date of letter.

9. D.M.Kneeland to H.Lunden, 8/26/1912, H. Lunden papers.

10. Biography of David Kneeland, unpublished.

11. C.Bigelow to H.Lunden, June 4, 1928

12. C. Bigelow to H. Lunden, May 15, 28, H. Lunden papers.

13. Letter, H. Lunden to C.A. Bigelow, October 1, 1927.

14. KB Financial Statement, December 31, 1928, box 3 at Bentley Library.

15. KBB Financial Statement, October 31, 1907.

16. Wayne B. Welch, *Early Life In the Johannesburg Area*, pages 68-70.

17. Fred White interview, March 5, 1988, letter March 2, 1988.

18. H.Lunden to C. Bigelow, 4/23/28.

19. H.Lunden to C.Bigelow, 6/19/28.

20. C.Bigelow to H. Lunden, March 18, 1904.

21. Abstracts of title, NE 1/4 of Section 26, T30N-R1E.

22. John D. Cress, *American Lumberman*, September 3, 1910, p.55, "Bay City".

23. Ward Estate Trustees' option, Jan. 29, 1912, H. Lunden files.

24. *American Lumberman*, March 30, 1912, p. 57. "The Saginaw Valley".

25. H.Lunden to C.Bigelow, June 19, 1928.

26. Lester Lunden interview, Sep 1, 1979.

27. Paul Thompson, Bay Trust Co. to KB Trust beneficiaries, May 19, 1954 (with Herman Lunden file), Bentley Library.

28. Kenneth L. Smith, *Sawmill: The Story of Cutting the Last Great Virgin Forest East of the Rockies*, (Fayetteville, Arkansas: University of Arkansas Press, 1986), Chapter 6.

29. Walter Thompson, KB teamster, interview by author, Jan. 15, 1986.

30. Herman Lunden files Bentley Library, box #5.

31. R.W. Stace to H. Lunden, October 5, 1925, H. Lunden files.

32. Lunden to Bigelow, Jan 30, 1925, H. Lunden papers.

33. Lunden to Bigelow, Dec 14, 1928, H. Lunden papers.

34. Proceedings, Department of Conservation, (Michigan) 1924,5,6, Bentley Historical Library, Ann Arbor, Michigan.

35. P.S. Lovejoy to H. Lunden, July 22, 1927, H Lunden files.

36. C.Bigelow to Department of Conservation, June 22, 1929, H. Lunden files.

37. C.Bigelow to H.Lunden, April 23, 1928, H. Lunden papers.

38. W. Wrape to H.Lunden, Oct 2, 1928.

39. H. Lunden to P. Kneeland, January 5, 1928.

40. Bigelow to Lunden, April 23, 1928, H. Lunden papers.

41. Fred J. White, KB storekeeper letter to H. Miller, March 27, 1984.

42. 1893 Builders' Dictionary, Train Shed Cyclopedia, Box 868, Novoto, CA 94947, has drawings of Russell logging cars.

43. Bigelow to Lunden, April 20, 1928; Lunden to Bigelow, April 23, 1928, H. Lunden papers

44. J.J. Stoner, Map of Bay City in 1879, and other maps, Bentley Historical Library, Ann Arbor, Michigan.

45. Correspondence between C.Bigelow and G. Cross, Oct 4, 1901, H. Lunden papers, Bentley Historical Library.

46. C. Bigelow to H. Lunden, August 30, 1926, H. Lunden papers.

47. C.Bigelow to H.Lunden, May 21, 1925, H. Lunden papers.

48. Arno Stevens, logger, interview by author.

49. John D. Cress, "Bay City," *American Lumberman*, September 3, 1910: 58-59

50. *Bay City Times Tribune*, June 13, 1925, page 1.

51. Kneeland-Bigelow Company advertising brochure.

52. C.Bigelow to H.Lunden, Feb.2, 1925.

53. George E. Butterfield, *Bay County Past and Present* (Bay City Michigan Board of Education 1957), page 90.

54. *American Lumberman*, March 9, 1912, page 71.

55. Lester Lunden.

56. Herman Lunden KB papers.

57. U.S. Department of Agriculture, Bulletin 1119.

58. H.Lunden to C.Bigelow, Oct 29, 1926, H.Lunden papers.

59. C.Bigelow to H.Lunden, March 18, 1904, H.Lunden files.

60. H. Lunden to A.C. Blixberg, Oct 15, 1925.

61. H. Lunden to C. Bigelow, July 13, 1928, C. Bigelow to H. Lunden, July 14, 1928.

62. H.Lunden to C.Bigelow, Sep 19, 1925.

63. C.Bigelow to G.Cross, 6/21/01, 7/7/01, 7/10/01, 9/11/01.

64. Fred J. White.

65. H.Lunden to C.Bigelow, May 16, 1928.

66. H.Lunden to C.Bigelow, May 22, 1928.

67. Fred J. White interview 1985.

68. Fred J. White letter, March 21, 1987.

69. Fred J. White letter, March 21, 1987, page 2.

70. Fred J. White letter, March 31, 1985.

71. Fred J. White interview 1984.

72. H.Lunden to C.Bigelow, 7/15/27.

73. Bryant, *Logging*, John Wiley & Sons, 1923.

74. Fred J. White.

75. Fred White interview, 1988.

76. Walter Thompson interview, Jan 15, 1986.

77. Fred J. White letter Mar. 31, 1985, interview Aug 9, 1985.

78. Arno Stevens interview, Jan. 30, 1988.

79. Photograph gallery, Sugarbowl Restaurant, Gaylord, Michigan.

80. Lester Lunden, comments on my 1969 draft, letter Feb. 16, 1969.

81. Fred White interview, March 5, 1988.

82. Walter Thompson interview, Oct. 20, 1987.

83. H.Lunden to C.Bigelow, Sep 27, 1924.

84. H.Lunden to E.E. Remington, Ford Motor Co., 12/16/24.

85. Freeman Parker, interview by author, July 19, 1993.

86. H. Lunden to C. Bigelow, Oct 13, 1927.

87. H.Lunden to C.Bigelow, Aug. 8, 1927.

88. U. S. Geological Survey map, Lewiston Quadrangle.

89. Arno Stevens, Historic Map of Montmorency County, *Montmorency County Tribune*, Atlanta, Michigan.

90. C.Bigelow to H.Lunden, Sep 8, 1927.

91. C.Bigelow to H.Lunden, May 4, 1925.

92. C.Bigelow to H.Lunden, Jul. 2, 1925.

93. Fred J. White letter, June 1986.

94. H.Lunden to C.Bigelow, Nov. 23, 1925.

95. H.Lunden to C.Bigelow, Dec 6, 1927.

96. H. Shearer, MCRR Gen. Mgr. to C.A.Bigelow, Nov. 12, 1925 placed new instructions in effect, including 5000 bd-ft minimum.

97. H. Lunden to C.Bigelow, Nov. 27, 1925.

98. W. Wrape to H.Lunden, 4/22/27.

99. Fred J. White interview, Jan 1988.

100. Fred J. White interview, 1988.

101. Lester Lunden, interview Aug. 21, 1978.

102. John D. Cress, *American Lumberman*, September 3, 1910:56.

103. Fred J. White interview, Oct. 30, 1983.

104. Fred J. White letter, March 21, 1987.

105. H.Lunden to C.Bigelow, Nov. 3, 1926, H. Lunden files.

106. Fred J. White interview, Oct. 30, 1983.

107. Arno Stevens interview, Jul 28, 1988.

108. H.Lunden to P.Kneeland, May 26, 1927.

109. Fred J. White letter, March 2, 1986.

110. Albert Stoll, *Detroit News*, May 24, 1925.

111. David Clink, *Montmorency County Tribune*, March 1969.

112. H.Lunden to C.Bigelow, Oct 13, 1927 & Nov 29, 1927.

113. H.Lunden to C.Bigelow, July 14, 1925.

114. *American Lumberman*, March 9, 1912.

115. H.Lunden to C.Bigelow, May 20, 1925.

116. Fred J. White interview, June 24, 1984, July 31, 1986.

117. *Detroit News*, January 15, 1928.

118. H. Lunden papers, Bentley Historical Library.

119. Fred J. White interview Sep. 25, 1979, letter Jul. 11, 1983.

120. R.J. Sack.

121. Fannie Manier, KB clerk, interview by author, August 22, 1984.

122. Marian S. Hook, schoolteacher, interview by author, 1985.

123. Lester Lunden interview, Oct. 25, 1975.

124. Fred J. White interview, 1984.

125. Lester Lunden.

126. H.Lunden to C.Bigelow, Nov. 3, 1926.

127. Walter Thompson interview, Sep 13, 1987.

128. H. Lunden to C.Bigelow, Jan. 7, 1928.

129. *Northwoods Call*, October 12, 1955.

130. Walter Thompson interview, Jan. 15, 1986.

131. Paul Thompson to KB Trust beneficiaries, May 19, 1954.

132. Labor reports, March 1929, H. Lunden files.

133. Paul Thompson to KB Trust beneficiaries, May 19, 1954.

INDEX